JOSEPH

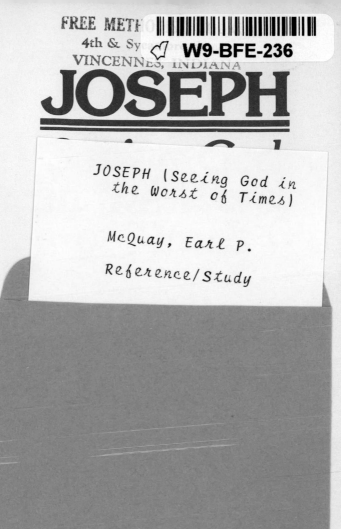

JOSEPH (Seeing God in
the Worst of Times)

McQuay, Earl P.

Reference/Study

ACCENT BOOKS
Denver, Colorado

A division of Accent Publications, Inc.
12100 West Sixth Avenue
P.O. Box 15337
Denver, Colorado 80215

Library of Congress Catalog Card Number 89-80409

ISBN 0-89636-256-6

Contents

AFFECTIONATELY DEDICATED

To

Pamela

our precious daughter.

May her dreams
always be God's dreams,
and her life
His fulfillment.

ACKNOWLEDGEMENTS

My heartfelt thanks is given to my wife, Rose, for suggesting and encouraging this study of Joseph, her favorite Biblical character. Also, appreciation is extended to Mrs. Mildred Sadler for reviewing my notes and providing helpful suggestions regarding composition. Finally, I am indebted to Miss Agness Barr, my indispensable secretary, for her diligence in typing the manuscript.

1

When Resentment Shatters Your Dreams

For the most part Jacob's sons were a wayward group. They broke his heart with their evildoings. But one was different—wise, sensible, loving, and submissive. Joseph brought great comfort to Jacob, and was his father's favorite son. Green with jealousy, the brothers ganged up on Joseph to rid themselves of him forever—or so they thought.

"He told on us! The brat gave a bad report on us to Dad!" That was the first thing that embittered the brothers against Joseph. The three sets of half brothers had been pasturing the flock, and young Joseph "brought unto his father their evil report" (Genesis 37:2). What do you suppose they were doing wrong? Could it be that a hint is given us some twenty years later, when Joseph sent his brothers home from Egypt with the single admonition not to quarrel

8

along the way " (Genesis 45:24)? One can imagine the word battles that probably were fought among the six sons of Leah, the two sons of Zilpah, and the two sons of Bilhah (Genesis 35:23-26). Whatever their iniquity, Joseph was compelled to report it to his father.

Joseph was not a mere tattletale. His motive in conveying to his father the report of his brothers' iniquity appears to have been good. Having nobler ideals than did his brothers, and having a spiritual kinship with his father, Joseph felt that Jacob should have these reports. It is possible, however, as some Bible students have suggested, that a trace of pride could have tainted Joseph's report. Joseph had the potential for being a spoiled brat. But God spared him from that lot by sending him away to Egypt as a slave.

Jacob's favoritism toward Joseph was another reason for the brothers' resentment. Jacob seems to have lavished extra love on the two sons of Rachel. Rachel was the wife of Jacob's choice, the only one he had married for love. Now an old man, Jacob had gone through many trials. His beloved wife Rachel had died on their way to Hebron and was buried near Bethlehem. Her two boys were left—Joseph, now seventeen, and Benjamin, an infant (Genesis 30:22-24; 35:16-20). Born to the beloved Rachel after her long period of barrenness, Joseph was especially loved by Jacob, who sought to protect him more than his other sons (see Genesis 33:2). Joseph's preeminence made him the object of jealous hatred.

As an expression of his affection for

Joseph, Jacob "made him a coat of many colours" (Genesis 37:3), a most unusual gift for a shepherd's son. This special coat was probably a tunic with sleeves. Ordinary tunics had no sleeves; but one with sleeves was a garment of distinction, perhaps implying exemption from manual toil, the special privilege of princes of that day.

Joseph's robe irritated his brothers. It flashed before them as a reminder of Jacob's favoritism. The brothers discerned in the special robe Jacob's intention to honor Joseph with the birthright forfeited by Reuben (Genesis 35:22; I Chronicles 5:1,2). The sight of Joseph wearing the coat goaded the brothers to hate him. The last act of their contempt would be the removal of the robe from Joseph and the dipping of the robe in the blood of a slain goat.

Jacob was unwise in letting it be seen how much he thought of Joseph, for it raised the envy and ill-will of the other sons. A father must beware of partiality. He should treat all of his children fairly and should extend his love to them equally.

Joseph's dreams were the third cause of his brothers' resentment (Genesis 37:5). It is good for a young man to dream. Accomplishments in this world usually are preceded by dreams. Dreams are seeds of glory. Dreams are a vital part of meaningful living. Some youths drift aimlessly through time and space, without a true motivation for living. They lack initiative and creativity. They lack vision.

God gave Joseph dreams of his future when he was only seventeen years of age.

Joseph dreamed that his brothers' sheaves bowed to his sheaf (Genesis 37:7). Again he dreamed that the sun, moon, and eleven stars made obeisance to him (verse 9). The meaning of his dreams was clear—his brothers and parents ultimately would bow to him. Joseph knew that his dreams had a special meaning and he was obliged to relate them to his brothers, as though it were the voice of God speaking through him. The implications of the dreams caused the brothers to despise him all the more.

There may have been something peculiarly offensive in the manner in which Joseph told his dream. Perhaps a certain amount of pride was revealed. But any cocky attitude Joseph may have had would be ameliorated in the years of waiting between the dreams and the fulfillment. Joseph was to be brought low before he would be exalted as his dreams indicated. He would have to wait fifteen years before he would stand in a position of honor above his brothers.

Dreams were one of the means God used to reveal His will to men prior to the completion of the canon of Scripture. But now the message of God to man is completed in Jesus Christ and is revealed in the Word of God (Hebrews 1:1-3; II Timothy 3:16,17).

We have the written Word of God to guide us and have no need of dreams. Our "dream" must derive from God's Word. Our responsibility is the reading and hearing of the Scriptures. The Word is our single rule for faith and living. It is, as someone said, "all we need to know about all we need to know."

Joseph's brothers "...hated him yet the

more for his dreams, and for his words"
(Genesis 37:8). Three reasons, therefore, are
given for the brothers' hatred of Joseph. His
integrity in advising his father of the brothers'
evil rebuked them. His reception of their
father's favor galled them. And his dreams
threatened them.

In one sense, Joseph's dreams of
supremacy over his brothers began to be
fulfilled as soon as they started to resent him.
Men hurt themselves much more by thoughts
of jealousy and hate than they hurt others.
Dr. S. I. McMillen, a medical missionary, has
poignantly amplified this fact:

> *The moment I start hating a man, I
> become his slave. I can't enjoy my work
> anymore because he even controls my
> thoughts. My resentments produce too
> many stress hormones in my body and I
> become fatigued after only a few hours
> of work. The work I formerly enjoyed is
> now drudgery. Even vacations cease to
> give me pleasure. It may be a luxurious
> car that I drive along a lake fringed with
> the autumnal beauty of maple, oak and
> birch. As far as my experience of
> pleasure is concerned, I might as well be
> driving a wagon in mud and rain.*
>
> *The man I hate hounds me wherever I
> go. I can't escape his tyrannical grasp on
> my mind. When the waiter serves me
> porterhouse steak with French fries,
> asparagus, and crisp salad, I swallow it,
> but the man I hate will not permit me to
> enjoy it.* [1]

The jealousy of Joseph's brothers led them to further evil. This is characteristic of sin, as James indicates: "For where envying and strife is, there is confusion and every evil work" (James 3:16). In Joseph's brothers are seen the effects of jealousy upon the *heart* ("they hated him," Genesis 37:4,5), upon the *mouth* ("could not speak peaceably unto him," Genesis 37:4), upon the *hand* ("stript Joseph out of his coat...took him, and cast him into a pit," Genesis 37:23,24), and upon the *life* ("all his sons...rose up to comfort him," Genesis 37:35). The sons pretended to "comfort" their father while they withheld from him the truth that could have brought him hope.

What must it have been like for Joseph to have all his older brothers against him? Their bitter resentment caused him great anguish of soul.

Have you felt the pain of being resented by others, perhaps even members of your own family? Have your dreams appeared to be crushed by human opposition? Be assured that God understands and behind the scenes is working out His good plan for you. Do not despair. Your loving Father promises to be there when all others fail you. In your disappointments God will bring forth the fruit of character and spiritual prosperity. As has been said, "It is the crushed grape that yields the wine!" Joseph is a marvelous example of the life guided by Providence to a meaningful end. He reached a higher level than rage against his persecutors; he ended up as their deliverer. His motivation was not a struggle against annihilation but a pursuit of

God's eternal blessing.

During those earlier years Joseph must have talked to God often about his circumstances. While he had the promise of becoming a ruler, he must have questioned why he experienced the pit, slavery, prison, and maliciousness. But these were a part of his training. In the pit and in the prison he learned to trust in God. God called Joseph to wait; and in his waiting he died to self-ambition, self-sufficiency, and self-glory.

Although Scripture does not indicate Joseph to be a type of Christ, we cannot help noticing a number of parallels between the two. Joseph's life falls into two periods—humiliation and exaltation; Christ's suffering was followed by His glory. Joseph was Jacob's favorite son; Christ was His Father's delight. Joseph was hated by his brothers; Christ was rejected by His own. Joseph was sold by his brothers; Christ was betrayed by Judas. Joseph was stripped of his coat; Christ was stripped of His robe. Though innocent, Joseph was imprisoned with two transgressors; the sinless Christ was crucified between two thieves. In accordance with their dreams, interpreted by Joseph, the chief cupbearer was released but the butler was hanged; one of the two thieves at Calvary turned to Christ in faith and was saved, the other rejected Him and was lost. Joseph's suffering was due to the sin of his brothers; Christ suffered because of the sins of mankind.

Joseph's period of humiliation in Egypt was used of God to save the entire nation of Israel; Christ's dying in humiliation is the source of our eternal salvation. Joseph eventually made himself known to his brothers and forgave and delivered them; Christ will reveal Himself to Israel one day and will restore her. In the end, Joseph's family and all of Egypt bowed before him; someday every knee will bow before Christ and every tongue confess that Jesus Christ is Lord, to the glory of God the Father (Philippians 2:11).

An important principle in God's dealings with all His own in all ages is taught us by the history of Joseph. It is the key to many a trial that we will meet as we journey through life. The principle is that humility goes before honor, bitter before sweet, the cross before the crown. "For our light affliction, which is but for a moment, worketh for us a far more exceeding and eternal weight of glory" (II Corinthians 4:17).

---

[1] S. I. McMillen, *None of These Diseases* (Charlotte, N.C., Commission Press, 1979), p. 72.

2
When Rejection
Exiles You

Jacob did not realize the grave consequences of a simple errand that he gave to Joseph. "Go...see whether it be well with thy brethren, and well with the flocks; and bring me word again" (Genesis 37:14). At the time, the brothers were pasturing their father's flock in Shechem, about fifty miles north of their home near Hebron. Joseph left home, not knowing that he would never return.

Like David, Joseph was sent by his father to look after the welfare of his older brothers. In God's purpose David was to return as a victor. Joseph was not to return at all, yet this too was a vital part of God's plan in the preservation of Israel. God doesn't always work in the same way. But in every life He does have a plan!

God was to allow Joseph, one of His choicest servants, to undergo severe trials. Although the ways of God are sovereign and beyond our finite understanding, we can discern that there may be great value in hardships because they prepare us for effective service. God sends trials not to impair us but to improve us.

Difficulties are not foreign to God's process of maturing a person for the task to which he is called. The spiritually wise have observed that "mature people are made not out of good times but out of bad times." A White House correspondent, noting the perils of a young, untested staff, declared that he believed no one should serve unless he is forty years old and has suffered at least one major disappointment in life. The men and women who have been greatly used of God first passed through the tests of life. It is after God breaks us that He uses us. After breaking the bread, Jesus fed five thousand people with it. Breaking results in multiplication.

Joseph was obedient to his father, knowing that this was the right thing to do. He undoubtedly knew about his brothers' hatred. He could have complained, "But they resent me; they may hurt me." Not Joseph. When his father asked him to go to his brothers at Shechem, he did not hesitate.

Joseph was persistent also. Had he lacked "stickability," he could have returned to his father with the report that he could not find his brothers at Shechem. But he searched until he found a man who had overheard the brothers discussing their plans and knew where they were. Joseph traced their steps to Dothan, about twenty miles north of Shechem (Genesis 37:17).

Suddenly, upon finding his brothers at Dothan, Joseph was thrust into the beginning of a series of great trials. He knew nothing of what he would be called upon to endure in the years that lay ahead of him. Whether his coat had been "many colors" or not, now his trials would be. The varied nature of the Christian's trials is recognized centuries later by the Apostle James: "My brethren, count it all joy when ye fall into divers temptations, knowing this, that the trying of your faith worketh patience" (James 1:2,3). The Greek word for "divers" means "many colored, variegated." James does not question the possibility of trials. He does not say "*if* you encounter," but "*when* you encounter various trials." That the Christian will have trials is certain. And the trials will be diverse, "many-colored."

On the fly-leaf of the Bible of a young minister, F. B. Meyer once wrote this admonition: "Never be startled at the temptations that assail, or the trouble through which your life travels. They are the predestined teachers of those deeper lessons for which men are waiting and which you can only learn by suffering and conquering." [1] When unexpected and upsetting things happen to us, we should not be taken aback. We know that they must have a meaning in the providence of God.

After our friends Allen and Isabel Fleece lost their teenage son, Ned, through an automobile accident, Isabel wrote of the tender dealings of Christ during the crisis. The lessons learned are summarized in the title chosen for her testimony, *Not By*

Accident. This Christian mother's heart responded beautifully to the sovereign overruling of God in a time of intense human sorrow and suffering: "Without faith the inevitable questions would come. Had we failed? Were we guilty in allowing Ned to drive? But by faith the inevitable answer stayed our hearts and held our minds. God had led us and him in every step that brought us to this hour and this place in our lives. God had not failed." [2]

The moment Joseph appeared on the horizon, his brothers put their heads together and decided to put him to death. "When they saw him afar off, even before he came near unto them, they conspired against him to slay him" (Genesis 37:18). They had been steaming with vexation over his dreams. Now they cold-bloodedly conspired to kill him. "And they said one to another, Behold this dreamer cometh. Come now therefore, and let us slay him, and cast him into some pit, and we will say, Some evil beast hath devoured him; and we shall see what will become of his dreams" (verses 19,20). They plotted not only the evil deed but what to say to their father about Joseph's disappearance.

Probably the greatest hurts we ever experience are those caused by persons we had most expected to be our faithful friends. A pastor friend wrote to me recently, "Our situation has not been easy. We have recently been hurt as never before—and it was by professing Christians. One might expect such from the world, but it seems to hurt so much more when it is by fellow brothers and sisters. God has been so good to us, though, and we praise Him even for these things."

It is difficult to speak of injuries that I have known when I was rejected or betrayed by those who were supposed to be friends. Perhaps you also have known such hurts and find it difficult to talk about them. It is enough that we simply commit these pains to our heavenly Physician, who assures us that He understands from His own experience. After all, He was "despised and forsaken of men; a man of sorrows, and acquainted with grief" (Isaiah 53:3).

Joseph's presence was a rebuke to his sinful brothers. The righteous person becomes an offense to the unrighteous. Christ spoke of believers as being "the salt of the earth" (Matthew 5:13) because their presence has an influence on society. The response to the savor of a godly life may be positive or it may be negative. Because the sinful world stands in rebellion against God, the usual reaction to the godly presence is to become offensive.

The sovereign working of the Lord is amazing. The Almighty's purposes would not be thwarted by the brothers. Though their act doubtlessly was to hinder the fulfillment of Joseph's dreams, the very method they used was employed by God to bring to pass those dreams.

Reuben was the first of only two brothers to manifest a spirit of compassion. He suggested that they cast Joseph into a pit rather than kill him. He hoped to return and release his brother and send him back to the father (Genesis 37:22). The distress that they were to suffer years later, the brothers would attribute to their present treatment of Joseph; and Reuben would recall his attempted interventions: "Spoke I not unto you, saying, against the child; and you would not hear? therefore, behold, also his blood is required" (Genesis 42:22).

As the oldest son, Reuben had the authority to stop the shameful treatment of his younger brother. But he was weak-willed. Rather than exercising his authority and demanding that Joseph be set free to return to their father, he tried to work out a scheme that would enable him to save face with his wicked brothers. Though his intentions were good, his action was not good enough.

When Joseph reached his brothers, the first thing they did was to strip him of his special tunic. Those brothers hated that coat! It represented their greatest cause of envy and hatred—their father's favoritism toward Joseph. Sometimes, a thing can stand between us and God's peace. It might be an automobile or a house that belongs to someone else. I knew of a situation in which it was a desk given to an administrator rather than to his rival fellow-worker. A material object, like Joseph's coat, can frustrate the soul unless the soul gets the victory over it. Is there some thing that is a stumbling block to you? Are you hoping that it will be destroyed? Peace will come when you get God's victory over the sin that is harbored in your heart in relation to it.

"They took him, and cast him into a pit" (Genesis 37:24). Joseph's prison was one of the deep pits dug in the hot, dry country to catch the rain water that falls only at certain seasons. Any effort to climb the shelving walls of rock would be useless. Suddenly he was cut off from the brightness of freedom above the ground and all his hopes came to an abrupt end. In the years that lay ahead of Joseph, much heartache and suffering were to serve as his schoolmaster.

While Joseph was in anguish in the pit, his brothers, with unbelievable callousness, sat down to eat a meal (Genesis 37:25). Probably while they ate, they continued to hear his cries for mercy from the pit. Many years later, when they were in a threatening situation in Egypt, they recalled the distress that they had caused Joseph and the manner in which he had pleaded with them for his life: "We are verily guilty concerning our brother, in that we saw the anguish of his soul, when he besought us, and we would not hear; therefore is this distress come upon us" (Genesis 42:21).

The appearance of a camel caravan of Midianite and Ishmaelite traders in the distance gave the brothers another idea— one that would accomplish their purpose of getting rid of Joseph and in addition would provide them some cash. Judah suggested that they sell Joseph into slavery, and the other brothers agreed.

Both Reuben and Judah wanted to save Joseph's life. They should have acted more positively in doing so, and should not have feared the other brothers. One must learn to do the right thing no matter what the crowd says or does. The united act of the brothers in rejecting Joseph proves that their character was not as good as Joseph's.

When my wife's oldest sister, Jenny, who had been like a mother to both of us, was stricken with incurable cancer, my wife often prayed, "Lord, heal our broken hearts." Has your heart been broken? Have you felt the pain that Joseph felt as he was removed from the security of all that he held dear in this world? Your Comforter is near in such a time. He can heal your broken heart.

I am fond of a beautiful china cup that my wife acquired in England. It is etched with delicate pink and burgundy roses and an eighteen-carat gold rim. My appreciation of the cup is enhanced by the fact that my wife's name is Rose. I understand that in the making of china, two types of stone are first finely pulverized, washed, and filtered. This material is mixed into a clay by being worked and kneaded. The complete mixture is molded and dried. After the painting is etched upon the piece, it is glazed and placed in a hot oven. A second firing is required to fix the enamel and gold colors. In a similar manner, the Lord allows us to be worked over and placed into the furnace of affliction in order that His divine image may be burned into us.

---

[1] W. Y. Fullerton, *F. B. Meyer, A Biography* (London, Marshall, Morgan and Scott, n.d.), p. 188.

[2] Isabel Fleece, *Not By Accident* (Chicago, Moody Press, 1965), p. 59.

Gen. 37. 28-36

3
When Separation Breaks Your Heart

How grieved was the heart of the young man, Joseph, as he was carried off to Egypt on that dismal journey. Every step took him farther and farther from his home, his kind father, and his younger brother.

The Midianite traders had valuable merchandise in Joseph, and they were sure of getting a good price for a lad like him in the land where all the house servants were slaves. The traders "brought Joseph into Egypt" (Genesis 37:28). Only this brief statement is given in reference to the ultimate destination to which Joseph was brought.

Reuben had planned to take Joseph home to his father. Being the firstborn, he was directly responsible for the lad. Having left the brothers for a season—perhaps to fulfill some chore related to the care of the sheep, or maybe to contrive some way of saving

Joseph—Reuben did not return until Joseph was gone. Dreadfully shocked, he tore his clothes—a sign of great grief—and ran to his brothers to tell them that Joseph was not in the pit. He was afraid to return to his father without Joseph. As the eldest, he was answerable for his young brother's safe return. Knowing that his father already had deep cause for displeasure against him, he cried, "The child is not; and I, whither shall I go?" (37:30).

The hardened brothers made up a story to deceive their poor old father. They dipped Joseph's tunic in animal blood and took it to Jacob (Genesis 37:31,32). Showing their father Joseph's stained coat, the brothers did not reveal that they had seen Joseph. They apparently wanted their father to conclude that Joseph had been slain by a wild animal before he ever reached them at the grazing grounds. Falling for their wicked deception, Jacob recognized the coat that he had given to Joseph and exclaimed in great grief, "It is my son's coat; an evil beast hath devoured him; Joseph is without doubt rent in pieces" (Genesis 37:33). Tearing his clothes and wrapping himself in sackcloth, the heartbroken father "mourned for his son many days" (Genesis 37:34).

How sad it is to see Jacob reaping the kind of falsehood that he himself had sown in his early years. As a young man he deceived his blind old father to gain the birthright. Jacob had sown deceit, and now he was reaping it. And bitter were the pains of that harvest! We must stand warned by the Scripture: "Be not deceived; God is not mocked: for whatsoever a man soweth, that shall he also reap. For he that soweth to his flesh shall of the flesh reap corruption; but he that soweth to the Spirit shall of the Spirit reap life everlasting" (Galatians 6:7,8).

Under the shadows of deceit, the sons pretended to comfort their father (Genesis 37:35). The sons withheld from him the only comfort that they could give to him—the truth that Joseph was alive. Jacob "refused to be comforted." And he said, "I will go down into the grave unto my son mourning. Thus his father wept for him" (Genesis 37:35). No man could speak comfort to a heart crushed as Jacob's was.

The loss of our son, Tim, has been the most painful experience of our lives. Completely committed to Christ, Tim longed to serve Him as a medical doctor. He was in his second year of medical school when he was killed in an automobile accident. That morning, while covering the stages of grief in my Pastoral Ministry class, I read from Leighton Ford's letter concerning the death of his son:

> *We grieve deeply over Sandy's death. The loss has been unexpected and far more crushing than we can express.... The day before surgery I prayed, "God, be good to my boy." God has been good, though not as we expected. We look forward to understanding more of why He chose to show His goodness in this way.*

Our hearts were deeply moved. I commented, "Men, I don't believe any one of us can fully realize the pain that this father has borne in the loss of his son!" I had no idea that on that very day I too would experience the agonizing torture of grief in the death of my son.

At lunch time, I received an emergency call from a doctor in Asheville, and learned that Tim had been hurt in an automobile accident. Friends drove us to Asheville, where we kept vigil for more than twenty-four hours until we received the shattering news that Tim was dead.

We had entered the darkest valley we could ever know, and we wondered whether we could ever see light again. Life without our beloved Tim has been unbelievably shattering. But our mourning is not despair. We are comforted by the assurance that Tim knew and loved the Lord Jesus, and that he is with our Lord today! We are aware, as Amy Carmichael states, that "all the pain is on thy side; all the joy is on his." Only someone who has experienced such a loss, we have found, is able to understand the agony of grief.

Imagine, for twenty years Joseph's brothers lived a lie! A person causes damage to his soul when he suppresses his conscience and will not heed its voice to uncover the truth. What he suppresses may be hidden beneath the surface of his conscious existence and he may not think about it for a long time; but subconsciously his soul is off-balance because of the improper treatment he has borne to his conscience.

Though separated from his earthly father, Joseph was not left alone; Joseph's God was with him. Though envious hearts and cruel hands had torn him away from his home, he had the assurance that none could hinder him from praying to his God.

God loves to walk with His people, even on their road of adversity. He is always there—in the wilderness of testing, in the cave of discouragement, in the shadow of death, in the furnace of trial, in the night of despondency. "For he hath said, I will never leave thee, nor forsake thee" (Hebrews 13:5).

The Lord never promises His children exemption from suffering in this life. Experiences of adversity are known by all men. But for the Christian, suffering carries with it the promise of good. In all that he experiences the believer can declare with John Newton, "Everything is needful that He sends. Nothing is needful that He withholds."

Though God does not withhold suffering from us, He does promise us the grace needed to bear it and His presence to enable us to prove His strength in our weakness. "God loves His people when He strikes them as well as when He strokes them."

What good does adversity do in our lives? Let's view some of the things that God accomplishes in us when He allows suffering.

Suffering exercises our faith. The story of Job shows his suffering to be a testing by Satan that was permitted by God to confirm and deepen the faith of His servant.

Amazingly, suffering does not lead to weakness; it strengthens us! Adversity can either make a person or spoil him. It can soften or harden his heart. Progress in life is made only in the face of opposition. It is the resistance of the air that makes the bird's flight possible. It is the resistance of the water against the propeller that aids the movement of the sea vessel. A person's spirit grows stronger, not as life becomes easier, but as testings and temptations are met and overcome.

A costly diamond is produced by the pressure and heat of the earth's elements. The crushed fruit gives tasty juice. The pressed flower releases the enchanting aroma. Pressure can be profitable. As A. B. Simpson wrote,

> *Out of the presses of pain,*
> *Cometh the soul's best wine,*
> *The eyes that have shed no rain,*
> *Can shed but little shine.*

Suffering strengthens our relationship with God. What Christian does not have to testify that extreme difficulty has driven him to prayer more than normal circumstances did? The experience of suffering introduces us personally to the meaning of weakness and impotence, and points us to the power of Christ, making us more dependent upon Him.

Afflictions show us our emptiness and God's fulness, our weakness and God's strength, our vileness and God's holiness. When the leaves fell from one of our hedges in the autumn, a bird's nest was exposed. It was unseen when the leaves were on in summertime. In prosperous times we do not see the nests of our hearts; but when our souls are stripped by adversity, we have a clearer vision of the God-man relationship. Truths that tended to be lost in the recesses of experience or to slip from the net of memory come alive in adversity.

Suffering matures our character. God aims to see His children grow up into spiritual maturity. By a sometimes painful pruning of the selfish and trivial things in our life, God refines our character and makes us more fruitful in His service. Jesus taught that the believer is like a branch that is totally dependent upon the vine (John 15:2).

In the world's atmosphere of sin, suffering apparently is a most potent factor in the development of the Christian. Moral and spiritual enrichment result from life's deepest troubles. C. S. Lewis says, "God whispers to us in our pleasures, speaks in our conscience, but shouts in our pains: It is His megaphone to rouse a deaf world." [1]

Suffering enhances our ministry. Paul declared that his imprisonment had turned out for the greater progress of the gospel (Philippians 1:12). God uses adversity to reveal His love. The doubts and despair of others can be lifted by their seeing in the believer the presence and peace of Christ when they suffer.

It is usually the one who has experienced the provocation of pain who can identify with others who are suffering. We don't always have to have the answers for problems in order to meet the needs of others. We may be like the little girl who had gone to the grocery for her mother. When her mother asked her why she was so long in returning home, she said, "I met my friend, Susie. Her doll was broken." "Did you stay to help her fix it?" asked the mother. "No," explained the little girl, "but I stayed to help her cry!"

When we have experienced difficulty, we are able to minister to others who have similar experiences later. Paul recognized this aspect of affliction when he spoke of the "God of all comfort; who comforteth us in all our tribulation, that we may be able to comfort them which are in any trouble, by the comfort wherewith we ourselves are comforted of God" (II Corinthians 1:3,4). A student shared with me this sustaining thought: "Yesterday's hurt is today's understanding rewoven into tomorrow's love."

Suffering produces future glory. "Earthly tears can become jewels for eternal diadems." Present suffering is the raw material of future glory. When we fix our gaze on the purpose and end of suffering, it will lose its bitterness. "For our light affliction, which is but for a moment, worketh for us a far more exceeding and eternal weight of glory" (II Corinthians 4:17).

Having passed through trials when we reach the presence of Jesus Christ, we will have something more to take with us that will magnify His glorious worthiness. Peter put it this way, "Wherein ye greatly rejoice, though now for a season, if need be, ye are in heaviness through manifold temptations: that the trial of your faith, being much more precious than of gold that perisheth, though it be tried with fire, might be found unto praise and honour and glory at the appearing of Jesus Christ" (I Peter 1:6,7).

Suffering accomplished its purpose in

Joseph's life, as the remainder of his story clearly demonstrates. Edith Hickman Divall's poem catches the whole point of the ultimate triumph of God in a life beset with many trials, like Joseph's:

The plan of the story is hidden,
Where only the Author can see;
And some of the parts, as I read them,
Seem strangely confusing to me.

I wonder why sorrow and hardship
Are needed to perfect the whole,
And why He must lead all His heroes
By perilous ways to the goal—

Why trial must touch them and parting,
Why sunshine must pass into shade—
And how from such unfinished fragments,
The final completeness is made.

Yet always I trust that these chapters
Will come to a beautiful close—
By patience and skill interwoven,
By Him who their mystery knows.

When meeting adversity, we should seek to learn the lesson that God has in it for us. And we should count on Him to bring us out of it victoriously as much better and obedient servants. Joy Ridderhof, God's radiant servant who founded Gospel Recordings, made a whimsical but wise statement: "Never get off in the middle of the tunnel."

[1] C. S. Lewis, *The Problem of Pain* (New York: Macmillan, 1971), p. 93.

4
When Slavery
Isolates You

With a heavy heart Joseph became a slave in a foreign land. He could have lost his confidence in the God of his fathers. He could have drifted into dejection and nihilism, and given himself over to passion. He could have resorted to shrewd schemes and aligned himself with corrupt political influences.

But wait, Joseph's response was uncommon. Although his circumstances were deplorable, he did not question the sovereignty of God. His confidence was not in his ability to understand his circumstances—his trust was in God. The calamity that befell him was enough to explode all his hope. But he did not give up.

It is the weak person who refuses to accept any limitations in life and is made petulant or frustrated by them. As a National League baseball umpire once said, "It is only the poor hitters, those who hit for low averages, who try to steal first base on you. They are the ones who kick dirt, and complain about the umpire's calls of balls and strikes. The great hitters, who know the strike zone, accept the judgment of the umpire." The Christian must learn to accept the calls that his Umpire gives him.

In handling adverse circumstances, we can curse God and turn away from Him; we can be angry with the world; we can indulge in self-pity; or we can entrust our souls to the sovereign Lord and believe Him for the fufillment of His will in us. The latter option is the one taught us in the Word of God. "When you don't know what to do, faith it!"

The purpose of Joseph's enslavement in Egypt, according to Psalm 105 was twofold: to test him and to preserve and strengthen his nation. Concerning the test the psalmist writes in verses 16 to 19:

Moreover he called for a famine upon the land;
he brake the whole staff of bread.
He sent a man before them,
even Joseph, who was sold for a servant.
Whose feet they hurt with fetters;
he was laid in irons,
Until the time that his word came:
the word of the Lord tried him.

God orders the events of the believer's life. Joseph was being tested, refined, and matured. He was being taught to stay himself upon God, to keep cheerful and charitable in frustrating circumstances, and to wait patiently for the Lord.

For more than three decades in Christ's service I have observed young men and women setting out upon a life of walking with God. In every case, I believe, there appeared a period of testing that followed the promising beginning. In some cases the disciples have met the challenge with firm commitment to their Lord and have come forth as stronger, more mature servants, capable of performing His work in their world. But in other cases the followers of Christ have succumbed to the test and have given up to the temptations of lust, materialism, or prideful ambition.

The account of Joseph's life fits into the background of Egypt under the Hyksos pharaohs, Semitic overlords who conquered Egypt but scrupulously observed Egyptian conventions. Their rule from 1710-1570 B.C. was established in the Delta, the great fertile wedge of Egypt formed by the spreading mouths of the Nile at the Mediterranean Sea. The Hyksos established an East Delta capital at Avaris (probably the same as the Greek Tanis and the Hebrew Zoan, Numbers 13:22).

In Egypt there soon was found for Joseph a master, "Potiphar, an officer of Pharaoh's, and captain of the guard" (Genesis 37:36). Potiphar no doubt selected Joseph in the market because of Joseph's age, appearance, and intelligence. But behind Potiphar's decision was the unwitting influence of Providence.

As soon as we are advised of Joseph's new situation as a slave in Egypt, we are told, "And the Lord was with Joseph" (Genesis 39:2). Here is the secret of Joseph's life.

Marvelous is the comfort of the truth that God is with us when He allows us to pass through the wilderness of testing. When we are in the wilderness, thinking we're all alone, not knowing why we're there or where we're going, God reminds us of His presence. He walks with us through the wilderness to see us through to the land of milk and honey, into the victory and blessing on the other side.

Usually God condemned His people for going to Egypt, the case being that they depended upon Egypt rather than the Lord for the provision of their needs. Egypt is in Scripture the symbol of the corrupt worldly system out of which God's people are redeemed and from which they are to separate themselves. But to be placed in Egypt by God is another matter. One must know who makes the decision. When placed in Egypt, in difficult circumstances beyond one's control, the child of God must accept his situation as from the Lord as a part of His good purposes. There he must stand the tests of Egypt in faithful commitment to God and must carefully keep himself unstained by the world (James 1:27).

Faithfully and zealously Joseph served God amid all the disadvantages of his place. As a result, "the Lord blessed the Egyptian's house for Joseph's sake; and the blessing of the Lord was upon all that he had in the house, and in the field" (Genesis 39:5). Very soon Joseph, a slave and an alien, rose to a position of favor in Potiphar's eyes (Genesis 39:2-4). He became Potiphar's personal valet. Potiphar had many servants, but he saw in Joseph something special distinguishing him from all the others. Joseph didn't simply blend in; he stood out.

Joseph was led of God into a waiting period in Egypt. Aren't we all compelled to do a lot of waiting? It appears to be the rule rather than the exception in life. We grow and we learn—not when things come our way instantly but when we are forced to wait. Waiting has become almost obsolete in our age of the microwave oven, crash diets, speedy print, and immediate cash. Our culture is adverse to waiting. It becomes a shock to our culturally infected system to enroll in God's spiritual life course that specializes in waiting. Often Scripture exhorts us to wait. "Wait on the Lord...wait, I say, on the Lord" (Psalm 37:14).

Waiting does not weaken us; it strengthens us. Isaiah tells us so: "But they that wait upon the Lord shall renew their strength; they shall mount up with wings as eagles; they shall run and not be weary; and they shall walk, and not faint" (Isaiah 40:31). The Hebrew word for "wait" in this instance means *to twist or to stretch in order to become strong*. As strands of plant fiber are stretched and twisted to form a strong rope, God stretches and strengthens us in the waiting periods of our lives.

What does it mean to wait upon the Lord? Consider the following five aspects of waiting: rest, trust, await, claim, and obey.

To wait upon God first means to *rest in God's comfort*. With his betrayal by his brothers, his separation from his father and homeland, and his enslavement in Egypt, Joseph scored a high number of stress points. But there is no indication that he became bitter. His faith in God sustained him.

Waiting, however, is never easy. David declared as he waited through terrible trials, "I am weary of my crying: my throat is dried; mine eyes fail while I wait for my God" (Psalm 69:3). Sometimes God draws the curtain in our lives, permitting times of shadow and even storms to accomplish His good purpose. He allows us to undergo trial, disappointment, and darkened days. And out of such experiences He causes us to bring forth love and tenderness, faith and compassion.

To know that no matter how bleak our circumstances may be we are not forsaken of God is cause for rejoicing. Our reaction to adverse circumstances may be faith's most crucial test. Our witness before the world is much more credible if we take adversity on the chin with faith born out of absolute trust in God's unchanging goodness. There is something triumphal about praise.

A second aspect of waiting upon God is to *trust in God's sovereignty*. The Lord before whom we wait is the personal, infinite God of the universe who works in our lives and is incapable of error. Our wait is rooted in the nourishing soil of His sovereignty that strengthens a wilting faith. Joseph's life in Egypt beautifully demonstrates trust in the sovereign Lord.

In waiting upon God, we refuse to take matters into our own hands. We will not interfere with God's working but will watch to see what He brings to pass. At such times we can identify with Phillips Brooks' statement, "I believe I have spent half my life waiting for God to catch up with me." Waiting involves trusting God to do what one cannot do himself.

To wait upon the Lord also means to *await God's working.* The dictionary defines "wait" as "to stay in a place or remain in readiness or in anticipation (*until* something expected happens or *for* someone to arrive or catch up)." For the believer to wait upon the Lord is to remain patiently in the place where God has placed him and to anticipate prayerfully the work of God to be accomplished in him through his experience there.

Joseph did not lose his dream. He knew that he was expected now to await God's timing in His life. Not knowing what the future held, he patiently committed himself to the will of God and awaited God's working. The story of Joseph's sufferings arouses the instinct of the reader to feel that all this is the prelude to some great manifestation of God's providence in the working out of Joseph's destiny.

An old Japanese proverb says, "With time and patience the mulberry leaf becomes silk." One of the fascinations of nature is the process from the mulberry leaf to a genuine silk kimono, but it is a long, long wait and takes time and patience. Strangely enough, the Latin root of patience, *pati*, means *to suffer.* The Greek word for patience, *hypomeno*, means literally *to stay under.* Taken together they give us this meaning: stay put, and suffer! Waiting upon God involves remaining in the trial or situation where God has placed you and "bearing with" it.

God's schedule is different from ours. When the psalmist commanded, "Rest in the Lord, and wait patiently for him" (Psalm 37:7), he used a phrase describing the period through which mothers go while they are awaiting the birth of a child. No matter how uncomfortable they may become or how inconvenient it may be, they must wait patiently. There is nothing else they can do. God has His own timing in answering our prayers; we must learn to await His schedule.

The fourth requirement of waiting is to *claim God's promises*. The Word of God is the basis of the believer's rest in God. He does not hope in his own ability or the ability of other persons. He does not hope in circumstances. But his hope is in the Word. "I wait for the Lord, my soul doth wait, and in his word do I hope" (Psalm 130:5). To rest on the Word of God is the only way we are able to sing in the darkness and rejoice in the midst of trial. Waiting upon God, we pray instead of worry; we seek instead of stray.

Joseph did not have a completed Bible such as we have today. He had only oral reports of God's revelation of Himself to the patriarchs and the memory of his father's spiritual instructions. But with the limited revelation that he did have, he held onto the promises of God.

Promises of the Word so often glibly quoted take on reality in the crucible of suffering. At such times God's words of comfort are like salve to an open wound. In trial periods, God's Word provides assurances with substance. While waiting upon God, we have the solid conviction that God's purposes cannot be defeated. We will not know the exact outcome but we are securely supported by the assurance that God allows no barriers to frustrate His purpose.

To obey God's guidance is a fifth need in waiting upon Him. Waiting does not mean that we have reached a spiritual standstill. Waiting is not simply the tapping of one's foot or the twiddling of one's thumbs. And it certainly is not simply gnashing the teeth in passive submission. Waiting includes the persevering pursuit of God's will within the present confines of adversity.

Joseph did not resign himself to despair in Egypt. He was faithful in whatever work became his responsibility. He accepted the tasks committed to him and fulfilled them faithfully.

To be faithful to the Lord in the areas in which we can exercise responsibility while leaving to His command the areas in which we have no control is a vital part of waiting upon God. The remedy for frustration is to turn toward what you can do and are permitted to do, rather than try to do what you cannot do and will never be permitted to do. In waiting we watch carefully for the direction of God in the steps that must be taken. We look for His guidance; and whatever glimmers of light He gives, we obey.

5
When Temptation
Batters You

Now in the midst of a great city, among men of strange faces and a foreign tongue, Joseph daily saw things that must have filled him with horror. The walls of his master's house would have been covered with pictures of creatures with hideous shapes that the people called gods. Though no one there knew Joseph's God, Joseph must have found security in pouring out his heart to his Father in heaven.

The "Upward Bound" program of Tauernhoff Bible School, a Torchbearer ministry in Schladming, Austria, involves stress camping in the Austrian alps. For the "solo," a student is left to live alone in the wilderness for forty-eight hours with only a piece of plastic, his Bible, and a pen and notebook for recording his thoughts during the time. Gernot Kunzelman, Director of Upward Bound, told us of one young lady who testified: "After being alone, and having no one to hear me talk but

God, I realized that I was an actor. I had spent my life putting on an act before people. But when I was alone with God, I found that I had to drop the act."

Separated from his godly father and the spiritual props of his homeland, Joseph was shut up to God alone. Would he stand the test? His faith there would either fall as a facade or withstand the paganism of Egypt.

The big test came in female form. Potiphar's wife was attracted to handsome young Joseph and persistently sought to lure him to make love with her. Suddenly he found himself facing the most subtle and volcanic temptation of his life.

Enamored of Joseph, the woman frequently attempted to entice him. "Lie with me" (Genesis 39:7), she would demand. But stoutly he resisted. The vile woman tempted him with every seduction in her power. Joseph declared that he would not betray his master's trust of him (Genesis 39:8,9). But more than the wrong against his master, Joseph knew that the sin would be wrong against God. "How then can I do this great wickedness, and sin against God?" he declared to the temptress.

She was determined to make a conquest. One day, when she saw that they were the only ones in the palace, she seized him in desperation. Frantically, Joseph ran out of the house, leaving his cloak behind.

The temptation of his master's wife brought out the marvelous character of Joseph. He was a man under control. His spiritual discipline defied appetites and passions. Now proved by fierce temptation, God's servant stood it and came out like pure gold.

Though there is a parallel between the two stories, there is very little reason to claim that the Biblical story of Joseph's temptation and "The Tale of the Two Brothers" in Egyptian literature are two versions of the same incident. This situation occurred often in the field of ancient literature. The Bible story is amazingly delicate and beautiful, whereas the other is crude and sensual.

The difference between the character of Joseph and that of his brother Judah is seen in the contrast between Joseph's victory over temptation here and the immoral shame of Judah with Tamar in the previous chapter (Genesis 38). Judah's sin with Tamar shows the world's influence invading the chosen community. On the other hand, Joseph's life shows how God carried a holy witness of His name to a heathen nation.

One must not be confused into thinking that temptation in itself is sin. It is sin to yield to a temptation, but it is not sin to be tempted. Jesus' temptation makes this obvious, for He "was in all points tempted like as we are, yet without sin" (Hebrews 4:15). We should be aware also that sexual desire in itself is not sinful. God has given us a sexual drive but has stipulated that it be controlled according to His will.

In Joseph's experience we see some of the characteristics of temptation. For one thing *temptation holds great inducements*. Not only was Joseph enticed to physical pleasure; there was an appeal to self-interest as well. The favor of this woman of prominence and position could have provided an excellent opportunity for advancement. Joseph could have been greatly flattered by the attraction of his master's wife.

The self-cult of situational ethics would reason, "Evidently Potiphar and his wife didn't have a good marriage relationship. She was needy. And Joseph was too: he was a virile young man who lacked a sexual companion. Joseph and this woman could have met each other's needs in a relationship meaningful to both and harmful to neither." So the world rationalizes. But Joseph knew that the only right thing for him to do was to stay as far as he could away from sin.

Temptation may be unpredictable. Joseph's was totally unexpected. It came at a time when things were going well for him. Also, the temptation came from an unexpected source. Little did he think that the wife of his own master would present such a test for him. Satan will strike when we least expect him to do so, and we must be ready at all times. As Paul wrote, "Wherefore take unto you the whole armour of God, that ye may be able to withstand in the evil day" (Ephesians 6:13).

Temptation strikes at a most vulnerable time. The allurement of the temptress came at a time in Joseph's life when sexual temptation would have been especially difficult to resist. Furthermore, the temptation struck hardest when "there was none of the men of the house there within" (Genesis

39:11). Joseph could easily have reasoned that no one would ever find out.

How opportune it would have been for Joseph to take up the offer for sexual gratification with a woman who made herself so available to him. Chances were that no one would ever know about it. There was no godly person in Egypt to influence him (or to "cramp his style"). No Bible was around to remind him of God and thereby convict him. Many a young person, away from home in the military, in school, or in business, has experienced strong enticement such as Joseph's. Away from home and godly influences, one becomes easy prey for Satan. Facades start to crumble and the reality of one's faith is tested.

Joseph's reaction to temptation was to have lasting effects. Had he yielded, the history of Israel could have taken a different course. What a person accepts or rejects, particularly in the realm of sexual temptation, will affect the rest of his life. Solomon warned: "Keep thy heart with all diligence, for out of it are the issues of life" (Proverbs 4:23).

Notice also that *temptation is persistent!* Potiphar's wife didn't give up. "And it came to pass, as she spake to Joseph day by day, that he hearkened not unto her, to lie by her, or to be with her" (Genesis 39:10). He kept his moral nature clean and free, and maintained spiritual manhood under pressure. "Day after day"—Satan doesn't let up!

From Joseph's experience we also learn the basic lessons for overcoming temptation.

To be victorious over temptation, we must

maintain a love for God. "How then can I . . . sin against God?" There is the source of Joseph's strength. He was motivated by love for God.

When the tests come, and they are sure to come, we must be sustained by a strong relationship with God. If you want God to stand by you in the hour of danger, you must keep near to Him at all times. Because Joseph stayed close to the Lord continuously, his God was close by to help him in the time of temptation.

To be a victor requires also that we *be filled with the Spirit.* The key to Joseph's life was expressed later when Pharaoh commented to his servants about Joseph: "Can we find such a one as this, a man in whom the Spirit of God is?" (Genesis 41:38). Only a God-indwelt person can continue to resist temptation as he did. The Holy Spirit lives in us and enables us to say "No" to sin.

Do you strongly feel temptations in your life? You can stand firm as Joseph did. How did he succeed? Certainly not by personal strength or any goodness of his own. He sought God's grace, and that was sufficient for him. As the Lord was with that young man, beset with strong temptations, and helped him to overcome the evil one, He has promised to be with you!

Overcoming temptation requires that we *trust the power of Christ.* Faith was the means of salvation and victory for Joseph and other Old Testament saints as it is for us today (Romans 4:1-25). Sin's power over us has been broken by Christ's death on Calvary (Romans 6:1-4).

God assures us of deliverance: "There hath no temptation taken you but such as is common to man: but God is faithful, who will not suffer you to be tempted above what ye are able; but will with the temptation also make a way to escape, that you may be able to bear it" (I Corinthians 10:13). Prayer, the power of Christ, and a redirected course are the "way of escape" that God has provided for us. When we are yielded to the Lord and are trusting in Him, we can pray to Him in faith and expect a power not our own to take hold and give victory when temptations come.

We are to *view sin in true perspective* if we are to overcome it. Joseph declared that to succumb to his temptation would be a "sin against God"! In David's repentance for adultery he declared, "Against thee, thee only, have I sinned, and done this evil in thy sight" (Psalm 51:4). When we understand sin to be a violation of God's holy character, we see what Paul meant in his statement that sin "might become utterly sinful" (Romans 7:13).

As his persecutors were considering the punishment of Chrysostom, one of the early church fathers, the suggestion of the dungeon was rejected: "No, he would appreciate the time alone with his God!" Death also was voted down: "He believes that he would go to be with his God!" Finally, a favorable response was given to the suggestion that might have been the most difficult one to achieve: "If there were some way that we could make him sin—that's the only thing that he is afraid of!" Oh, that this were true of every one of God's children!

Determine to stand against sin, as Joseph did. This is another requirement for victory. A basic need in overcoming temptation is to truly want to overcome. We must not deceive ourselves into praying for victory when deep down in our hearts we cherish the sin and do not truly want to escape from it.

Joseph determined from the beginning that he would not sin. He took a strong stand against the continual temptation from the very first. He would have been easy prey if he had even considered the possibility of committing fornication. As Christians, we must determine that we will not yield to temptation and bring dishonor to God.

Sin has its beginning in man's lust. When James said that each one "is tempted, when he is drawn away of his own lust and enticed" (James 1:14), he used a word that means *dragged away*, a word used in Greek literature for drawing a fish out from under a rock. The responsibility for sin lies in man's own evil desire. The tempter would be helpless unless there were something in man to which he could appeal.

Learning to *apply the Word of God* is another aid to overcoming temptation. Joseph did not have Scripture as we do. His knowledge of sin and righteousness was based on the teachings of the patriarchs. He was true to the principles that he had been taught. We have the whole Bible. Consult a concordance or Topical Bible for appropriate Scripture references that speak directly to your particular needs. Memorize the verses. Learn to obey the first promptings of the Holy Spirit in the face of temptation. When the mind skips into forbidden territory, deal with the thoughts immediately. Reject the thoughts, and turn to thoughts of Scripture appropriate to helping you overcome the temptation.

Joseph's experience vividly teaches us another lesson in overcoming sin: *flee from temptation.* Joseph refused to listen to his temptress even "to be with her." One must be careful not even to allow himself to be in a position of temptation.

Joseph was in the house of Potiphar only when he had duties to perform there. There is no indication that he lingered there without cause. "Joseph went into the house to do his business" (Genesis 39:11). He exercised caution against being near the mistress of the house except when he absolutely had to be. We cannot depend on God to give us strength to resist temptation if we willfully and enjoyably walk in the area of temptation.

When temptation struck Joseph he fled! "And he left his garment in her hand, and fled" (Genesis 39:12). He immediately got out of the area of temptation. We cannot toy with temptation. It is not cowardly to run from sin. Paul wrote to Timothy, "Flee also youthful lusts: but follow righteousness, faith, charity, peace" (II Timothy 2:22). Flight is the only safety for temptations of lust. To linger would be to fall. As someone has said, "Kill the serpent; don't stroke him."

To *concentrate on the good* is a final guideline to victory over temptation. Joseph lived with God even though he was a slave in the house of Potiphar. He was able to stand victoriously against temptation because his mind had not been dwelling on sex. He occupied his time with appropriate things.

Christ's prayer for His own was: "They are not of the world.... I pray not that thou shouldest take them out of the world, but that thou shouldest keep them from the evil. They are not of the world, even as I am not of the world" (John 17:14-16). In dealing with our besetting temptation, we must learn how to replace the evil with good. We should pray for the opposite of what we are tempted to do and then concentrate our efforts to occupy our lives with the opposite good.

Joseph was "salt" and "light" in Egypt. Rather than letting Egypt shape him after its mold, he stood above Egypt, in God, and manifested God to Egypt. To maintain purity does not necessitate the Christian's withdrawal behind a pharisaical robe of piety and psychological isolation from the rest of the world. To be Christlike in attitude and behavior, one must maintain personal integrity while at the same time engaging in relationships with all kinds of people. This is the only way the Christian can put the non-Christian in touch with Christ. To be involved in the world as Jesus was is to interact with the world on issues of current interest in an intelligent and responsive way, without accommodating one's view to the point of compromise on basic issues. Always, rather than lowering our own standards or compromising our convictions, we must seek to raise the sights of others to face the issues of life in the light of eternal truth. Joseph is a marvelous example of one who was faithful to God in the midst of a godless society.

6
When Slander
Devastates You

"Hell hath no fury like that of a woman scorned!" Utterly frustrated in her "Waterloo" attempt to seduce Joseph, the temptress vowed revenge. She raged against him with false accusations, attempting to discredit him by claiming that he had forced his attentions upon her.

Potiphar's wife accused Joseph first to the servants of the house. Hoping to arouse their anger against Joseph, she reminded them that he was a Hebrew (an abomination to Egyptians) and cast aspersion on her husband for having Joseph in the house to begin with (Genesis 39:14).

Later she accused Joseph to Potiphar upon his return. The same report was given to him, "The Hebrew servant, which thou hast brought unto us, came in unto me to mock: and it came to pass, as I lifted up my voice and cried, that he left his garment with me, and fled out" (Genesis 39:17,18). Producing the coat as evidence, she hoped to make her husband angry enough to kill Joseph.

Potiphar's anger burned (Genesis 39:19). He hurried Joseph off to prison. Because Joseph was a slave, he was given no opportunity to prove or to plead his innocence. Potiphar may have had some question in his mind about Joseph's guilt, for he did not kill him. Perhaps the favor shown Joseph was due both to Potiphar's knowledge of Joseph's integrity and his knowledge of his own wife's wickedness. Yet the circumstantial evidence was present, and Joseph was strongly incriminated.

Though Joseph's promising career appeared to be utterly wrecked, he was to learn that imprisonment would prove to be a part of God's mysterious plan. Joseph no doubt found it difficult to understand what was happening in his life, but God knew what He was doing. What a setback his imprisonment appeared to be for Joseph! It had seemed that he was making some progress toward the fulfillment of his dreams as he served over Potiphar's household. But now the bottom had fallen out, and he was in prison.

A problem most difficult to endure is slander, an untrue statement damaging to the character or reputation. I suppose the first time I felt this type of pain in my ministry was when a member of my congregation heard me state in a sermon that many of our people lacked spiritual gumption; he then spread the word in the community that I had called all our church members ignoramuses. He had looked up the word "gumption" in a dictionary, which somehow used the word "mind" in its definition.

A few deacons in another church established a pattern of stipulating a certain five worldly taboos from which applicants for membership were asked to abstain before they would be recommended to the church for membership. Though I agreed that the five areas were not appropriate for a committed Christian, I held that one's profession of faith in Christ as Saviour and Lord was the basis of consideration; and I viewed the commitment requirement to be legalistic. The men spread the word that I was a liberal; and my ministry in the church and community was damaged. Fortunately the situation was redeemed when the congregation took a Scriptural stand on the issue; but unfortunately several families were lost by the church.

Through the years even more devastating experiences have been mine, which I am not free to write about. But I have found this to be true of many Christians. It happens sooner or later to anyone who is committed to serving Christ. In fact our Lord said, "Woe unto you, when all men shall speak well of you" (Luke 6:26). Slander is a major weapon of Satan, and "we are not ignorant of his devices" (II Corinthians 2:11).

Joseph's plight at the hand of a false accuser takes a thousand shapes as it is repeated in the lives of God's children today. You may be misunderstood, falsely accused, slandered, and perhaps even persecuted. How will you handle such treatment? Observe Joseph for some helpful ideas.

Joseph's first step in handling slander was

to *remain faithful to the Lord*. He stayed himself upon God. The psalmist reminds us of the security that such reliance brings: "In the multitude of my thoughts within me thy comforts delight my soul" (Psalm 94:19).

Joseph refused to be unfaithful to God, no matter how bad his circumstances were. Loyalty to the Lord is the outstanding characteristic of his life. If you face human assault, don't let it turn you away from God. Think upon His goodness to you in past times and trust Him for His future working. Search the Scriptures for encouraging promises to those in trouble and sorrow. Evil may have temporary victories, but God's purpose will prevail.

A second lesson Joseph teaches for handling slander is to *trust the Lord to be your defense*. No indication is given whether Joseph ever attempted to defend himself when he was cast into prison. He may have realized that no defense would do him any good under the circumstances. Probably he was given no opportunity for self-defense. But he knew that he was innocent; and again he committed his soul to God.

Better to have a clear conscience and be in prison than to be wicked and rich and free! If one is to suffer, it is best that it be undeserved rather than the reward for wrongdoing. Peter makes this clear: "For this is thankworthy, if a man for conscience toward God endure grief, suffering wrongfully. For what glory is it, if, when ye be buffeted for your faults, ye shall take it patiently? but if, when ye do well, and suffer for it, ye take it patiently, this is acceptable with God" (I Peter 2:19,20).

Sometimes God places us in an impossible situation so that He can reveal to us our own wickedness and utter inability to cope with life's situations. It is then that we are in the best position to see God bring His victory and release. Luther's assistant, Melanchthon, made this observation: "Trouble and perplexity drive me to prayer, and prayer drives away perplexity and trouble."

Do not try to live with misunderstanding and bitterness weighing on your mind. Turn the matter over to God and pray, "Lord, they misunderstand me. I have been falsely accused, and no one comes to my defense. I'm right, but they don't see that. Please take over and help me." Then rest in the knowledge that He has taken over. Our lives must be controlled by the love of Christ within us and not by what others think of us and to do us.

Victor Frankl, who experienced a nightmare of deep suffering in a German concentration camp, once stood stark naked before his tormentors. One of them, noticing his wedding band, stepped forward to remove this last symbol of humanness. "You can take everything away," Victor solemnly responded, "except one thing: my freedom to react to you in a Christian manner." Actions tell us what a person can do, reactions tell us what he is. Joseph proved what he was by his reactions.

Abraham Lincoln once remarked regarding his critics: "If I were to try to read, much less answer, all the attacks made on me, this shop might as well be closed for any other business. I do the very best I know how—the very best I can; and I mean to keep doing so until the end. If the end brings me out all right, what is said against me won't amount to anything. If the end brings me out wrong, ten angels swearing I was right would make no difference."

In sober retrospect of eighty years, a venerable Christian has testified: "I have often been wrongfully attacked, but have never attempted to defend myself. I have borne in silence and committed my cause to God and there has never been a wrong done me that has not been rectified."

Has someone said false things about you? Have your plans been all upset? Are you crushed and weary? Take your case to the highest court—the court of heaven—"casting all your care upon him, for he careth for you" (I Peter 5:7). Depend upon Him to clear your name. You may have to wait for months—in some cases, years—for God to vindicate you. But His time will come. You can count on it! "Rest in the Lord, and wait patiently for him" (Psalm 37:7). God may be testing you for some reason; and He will keep the fire on until His purpose is accomplished, rather than ruin the product He is producing.

We may learn another lesson from Joseph in surviving slander: *Seek the Lord's guidance.* We have responsibilities that we must continue to fulfill, and we will need His grace and guidance to do so. David prayed, "Teach me thy way, O Lord, and lead me in a plain path, because of mine enemies" (Psalm 27:11). It is easy to "lose our cool" and to make the wrong move in times of tribulation. But when we keep our eyes on the Lord He will keep us "level-headed," for He will lead us "in a level path."

A pilot who was inexperienced in instrument landing was lost in a fog. The station tower decided to bring him in on radar and began to give him directions from the ground. When the pilot remembered with fright a certain tall pole in the flight path, he was reluctant to follow the instructions of the tower. From the tower came a command with dictatorial authority: "You obey *instructions*; we will take care of *obstructions*." Joseph was not immobilized by obstacles. We too must go on. We can't quit. We are to obey the light we have until we get more. Obey instructions; God will take care of the obstructions!

While trusting God to right the wrong in our situation, we must move on to the work that God has committed to our trust. We must not allow the foe to cause us to stand still or lose ground. Joseph did not sulk at his unhappy lot and become shiftless in new responsibilities. He was patient and long-suffering. And he fulfilled the trivial prison tasks as faithfully as he had served Potiphar's household. This faithfulness qualified him for receiving the next opportunity in God's plan.

7
When Ingratitude Dashes Your Hopes

Impeccably innocent, Joseph was carried off to a prison. The prison was a "round house," indicated by the Hebrew noun construction. It probably was a famous round tower where prisoners connected with official life were housed—"a place where the king's prisoners were bound" (Genesis 39:20). Partly a subterranean dungeon (Genesis 41:14), the prison probably rose above the surface of the ground and was surmounted by a dome roof. In the beginning of his prison life Joseph was subjected to extremely harsh treatment. According to the psalmist, Joseph's feet were hurt with fetters and he "was laid in iron" (Psalm 105:18).

Joseph's tests till now were before people—his brothers, Potiphar, and the temptress. Now he faced the test of solitude, and Satan attacked his mind. Alone in prison Joseph had time to think. No doubt he reflected on all the experiences of his life till now; and he sought to interpret their meaning. I like an expression Britishers use: "Get everything sorted out." It means the same as the American expression, "Get it all together." That time comes in life when we are pressed to "sort things out" and "get it together." Joseph arrived at that position in the "round house."

Joseph did not experience sheer suffering alone. He experienced God's tempering grace in the innermost areas of his spirit. Whatever his mental exercises were, one thing is clear—he maintained his faith in God.

Your situation may be similar to Joseph's. What turmoil of soul you will experience if you concentrate on your circumstances rather than upon God. The solution is wrapped up in a maxim shared with me by a student many years ago:

When we look without, we are distressed;
When we look within, we are depressed;
But when we look to Him, we are at rest.

"Songs in the night" don't come to us when all is going well. We receive night songs in places like strange lands, prisons, and solitary, dark corners. Joseph learned the meaning of human loneliness. God used this time of isolation to prepare him for his later ministry to others.

Twice we are told of Joseph in prison that the Lord was with him (Genesis 39:21,23). What a tremendous difference this made in his life. It is better by far to be in prison with the Lord than a free man without Him!

A missionary who had been forced out of China received a letter from China—an airform covered with Chinese characters. The letter was from a man who had worked with him, a man who knew the Lord and was a faithful servant of Christ. But the letter was so shocking; it praised the People's Republic and all that Chinese Communists portrayed as advancement in their country. "This isn't the man I knew," the missionary declared as he read the letter with voice breaking. "This isn't the man I worked with. Something has happened to him." He was about to fold up the letter when in the lower corner he noticed a smudge. Looking at it carefully, he saw that it was the Chinese character for "Immanuel— God with us." Suddenly it dawned on him that the friend had written in praise of communism in order that he might get the letter through the censor—to send one word of news, written with the single hair of a writing brush, "Immanuel, God with us." That's the best news of all!

Psychologists generally recognize despair to be the effect of repeated disappointments. Wouldn't you think that Joseph had had enough disappointments by now to lead him to despair? But what spiritual resilience we witness in this young man! His secret? God! In prison Joseph was safe in his Father's care. Though physical darkness surrounded him in the dungeon, he was enveloped in spiritual light. Not only was he surrounded by prison walls; he was garrisoned by the God of peace.

The prison experience was a vital part of

God's divine plan for Joseph. Frustrations and detours are used of God for His good purposes in our lives. It has been said, "If you're not churning, you're not learning." Pressure is good for us. The most creative time in America's history, it has been reported, was December 8, 1941. Many innovations today are a direct result of the research that grew out of the years following Pearl Harbor.

Though guiltless, Joseph suffered ignominy, but his prison became a high road to honor. Both the life of our Lord and the teaching of the New Testament designate humiliation before exaltation. Though there is no music in a rest, there is the making of music in it. As in a great concert, the music of our life is broken off here and there by "rests." They are carefully noted by our Conductor, who beats time with the rests as certainly as He does with the musical notes, tying them together as if there were no breaking places at all. God strikes our "rests" fully and clearly. They are necessary in His complete musical score.

In medieval times the goldsmith had a unique method of determining when the precious metal had been purged of all extraneous matter by the refining fire. It is reported that he would look intently into the seething, molten mass, while increasing the heat more and more. A smile would at last lighten up his perspiring face when the goldsmith could see his face reflected in the molten mass of gold. He knew that the gold was purified when he saw his face mirrored. Into our lives God peers intently, while He allows His purifying fires to burn. When He sees the image of His dear Son reflected in our lives, He knows the refining fire has accomplished its intended purpose.

Joseph was in prison for more than two years (Genesis 41:1). Basically he spent the years waiting—waiting for God to do His work. The major accomplishment of that time was not Joseph's work for God but God's work in Joseph. He was being prepared for the future.

Dr. Victor Frankl, psychiatrist and neurologist, who was a survivor of Auschwitz and three other Nazi death camps, said the lesson he learned in the camps "was that those prisoners most oriented toward the future, those who clung to some shred of meaning, were the most likely to pull through." The same report came out of the Korean Communist camps. The U.S. soldiers who could victoriously withstand the brainwashing were those who had a firm faith.

God did not let Joseph remain in irons. Because the Lord was with Joseph, he was given "favor in the sight of the keeper of the prison. And the keeper of the prison committed to Joseph's hand all the prisoners" (Genesis 39:21,22). He knocked the chains off Joseph and made him the supervisor of the other prisoners. Joseph was not a complainer, a gloomy grumbler who deplored his condition. His hopeful and confident spirit captured the attention of his superiors.

Joseph never got a promotion by compromising his convictions. God blessed him by guiding men to see his quality of character. Possibly the keeper of the prison, because of the close proximity of the prison to Potiphar's palace, had been acquainted with Joseph prior to his imprisonment. He may have known of Joseph's character and of his innocence of the crime charged against him.

While he served in the round tower, Joseph had two new prisoners committed to his supervision. Both were high officials of great rank and importance in Pharaoh's palace. They were committed to prison until their case could be investigated.

The "butler," or cupbearer was overseer of the royal vineyards and the cellars, with undoubtedly hundreds of people under his supervision. The "chief baker," the second official now thrown into prison, had complete superintendence of the meals for the royal table.

"Wherefore look ye so sadly to day?" Joseph inquired one day of the two officials now with him in prison (Genesis 40:7). Who would expect prisoners to be anything but sad? But Joseph was discerning. He detected a unique heaviness in the countenance of his fellow prisoners.

Joseph was sensitive to the feelings and needs of others. That's the way God's man is! The Christian is taught, "Look not every man on his own things, but every man also on the things of others" (Philippians 2:4). One positive action one can take when he feels loneliness is to reach out to someone else who has a need. Joseph helped others in their trouble as though he had none of his own.

The training of Joseph's prison years influenced his sympathies more than anything else could. It may be that his quick recounting of his dreams to his brothers had shown a lack of sensitivity to their feelings. In prison he would come to realize that he was not the only person whose emotions had a right to be regarded. Through his own suffering he was made tender to the sufferings of others.

Joseph's faithfulness in his responsibility for the prisoners is indicated by his sympathetic inquiry into the cause of the two men's sadness. He did not wait for some great occasion to serve. He observed that two men were sad, and he got involved in helping them. Little did he realize that this very act would be a steppingstone used of God to get him into Pharaoh's palace two years later. God designs our contracts; we should make the most of them.

Often I have sought to impress upon young people in college preparation for Christian service not to think of ministry as something off in the future somewhere but to view their lives as presently involved in ministry. To the degree that one is faithful to lay hold upon opportunities presently available to him, he will receive greater opportunities in the future. Jesus indicated this principle when He declared, "He that is faithful in that which is least is faithful also in much: and he that is unjust in the least is unjust also in much" (Luke 16:10).

For the two celebrated prisoners to dream similar dreams in the same night obviously was providential. Observing their depression the following day, Joseph inquired as to the cause. They told of dreams that they could not understand. They felt that some deep meaning was hidden in what had come to them so vividly in the night.

Joseph volunteered to aid the men in discovering the import of their dreams, indicating that the God he served was the giver and the interpreter of dreams. "Do not interpretations belong to God? Tell me then, I pray you" (Genesis 40:8), he urged. Joseph's expression regarding God's work through dreams reveals how he felt about his own dreams. He harbored no doubts about his youthful dreams. His confidence in God had not been shaken even though he did not understand how God was working out His plan.

Speaking as an inspired interpreter, Joseph defined the cupbearer's dream of squeezing grapes from a productive vine of three branches and placing the cup of wine in Pharaoh's hand. Within three days the cupbearer would be freed and would resume all the privileges of his office.

So confident was Joseph that his interpretation of the dream would come true that he requested a return of kindness from the cupbearer. Faith seized the opportunity! "But think on me when it shall be well with thee, and shew kindness, I pray thee, unto me, and make mention of me unto Pharaoh, and bring me out of this house" (Genesis 40:14). Joseph refused to surrender to morbid depression. He did not complain; he trusted! He wanted to be free that he might experience the full will of God in his life. "Remember me," he requested. He refused to give up.

The chief baker was anxious for Joseph to interpret his dream also. In his dream, birds

were eating from three baskets of baked food
that he was carrying on his head to Pharaoh.
Such a scene probably was common in
Egypt, where the baskets of food were
carried across open courts to the dining
room, and carnivorous birds would swoop
down to steal away the food. Birds swarmed
in large numbers in Egypt, where they were
held sacred and were protected by law
against destruction.

Though the news was tragic, Joseph
honestly interpreted the dream: "Yet, within
three days shall Pharaoh lift up thy head from
off thee, and shall hang thee on a tree; and
the birds shall eat thy flesh from off thee"
(Genesis 40:19). No doubt it was painful for
Joseph to communicate such dismal tidings
to the baker. But he was faithful to his
responsibility to pass on what God had
revealed to him.

Time proved that Joseph's interpretations
of the dreams were true. Three days later
Pharaoh celebrated his birthday, a holiday
occasion of great magnificence. Perhaps
Pharaoh missed his cupbearer and chief
baker at the feast. He inquired into their
cases that he might settle them. Things
happened as Joseph had predicted—the
cupbearer was restored and the chief baker
was hanged.

Hearing of the cupbearer's release, Joseph
was stirred with hope that he would be
remembered before Pharaoh. But again his
hopes were dashed to pieces. The cupbearer
forgot Joseph (Genesis 40:23). In his prosperity he overlooked the one who had be-
friended him in adversity. He forgot Joseph

completely for two whole years. How ungrateful!

Men are so prone to forget. When things go well for them it is easy for them to forget those who helped them when they were in tight spots. I have known the feeling of being forgotten by one whom I helped. Perhaps you've borne the same experience. Ingratitude hurts.

Christians must learn to reciprocate: thus the thirty-four "reciprocal commands" of the New Testament such as "love one another," "be kind one to another," and "serve one another." Napoleon once said, "I love nobody, not even my own brothers." It is not strange, therefore, that at the end of his life, on his rock prison in the South Atlantic, he said, "I wonder if there is anyone in the world who really loves me."

More waiting! How dreadful! And Joseph had no idea how long it would be. But he would not be overcome by discouragement. He continued to perform his prison duties faithfully and to wait patiently before God, never knowing what God would do. Disappointment is the piercing tip of Satan's arrowhead. To resist his arrow, do not be open to disappointment. Disappointment wedges the way for discouragement and ultimately leads to despair.

Joseph withstood disappointment by keeping his eyes on God rather than on circumstances. God was following His own schedule and Joseph continued to trust Him. Though man forgets, God does not.

An illustration has been told regarding the promise to Israel, "I will restore to you the years that the locust hath eaten" (Joel 2:25). In one place that was eaten by locusts, the locusts all died afterwards and fertilized the ground. The next year a bumper crop resulted. In Joseph's ostensibly lost years God was accomplishing His purpose. Divine Providence has a mysterious way of working wonders without seeming to work at all!

A young friend recently told me of the Lord's working in his life during the summer, which he spent living with missionaries presently at home in the States. "I've been to conferences where I got my battery recharged. But this summer the Lord gave my motor an overhaul. Some parts He cleaned, and some parts He threw away and replaced." Joseph's experience in prison must have been something like that. It's difficult to know what areas of need he had; he always appears to be flawless. But I'm sure that God was doing something in his life to better prepare him for his future task.

8
When Prosperity Shines On You

The long night is over, Joseph. The day of glory has come at last. Yesterday you lay forgotten in the dungeon; but today you will stand on the steps of the throne. The companion of criminals is about to become the counselor of the king—and after that, the prince among princes.

Because Joseph was faithful to God in days of insignificance, he is ready now to meet the greater challenge. The Lord was with him in the thirteen years of darkness; He will be with him now in bright days of prosperity.

Two full years after the release of the chief cupbearer, Pharaoh himself was disturbed by two mysterious dreams. Seven well-fed cattle grazing in a meadow by the Nile were eaten up by seven thin cattle that came up out of the Nile. Again, seven good ears of grain on one stalk were swallowed up by seven thin ears.

Pharaoh summoned all who might be able to interpret his dreams. "And it came to pass in the morning that his spirit was troubled; and he sent and called for all the magicians of Egypt, and all the wise men thereof; and Pharaoh told them his dream, but there was none that could interpret them unto Pharaoh" (Genesis 41:8). The Egyptian wise men, through long practice, were expert in devising suitable answers to get them out of any difficulty. But Pharaoh's dreams baffled their united skill.

When no one was found to interpret Pharaoh's dreams, the sluggish memory of the cupbearer finally was stirred. God's mastercontrols ignited the cupbearer's memory. Suddenly aware of his thoughtless forgetfulness and ingratitude, the cupbearer was conscience-stricken. He exclaimed to Pharaoh, "I do remember my faults this day" (Genesis 41:9). He told Pharaoh of Joseph's ability to interpret dreams.

Pharaoh summoned the Hebrew slave at once. "Then Pharaoh sent and called Joseph, and they brought him hastily out of the dungeon: and he shaved himself and changed his raiment, he came in unto Pharaoh" (Genesis 41:14). Egyptian custom dictated that one must be shaven and dressed in linen for an appearance at court.

Aren't you encouraged when you see how God's faithfulness came through for Joseph? Joseph was kept safe in the midst of all the hatred and cruelty of his brothers. The scandalous slander of his accuser could not damage him. The ungrateful forgetfulness of his fortunate fellow-prisoner would only serve God's timetable.

God's care for each of His children is clearly promised throughout His Word. But we are so prone to doubt His presence when we fall on difficult times. Some of us may be guilty of being what someone has described as "elevator Christians"—when things are good, they go up; when circumstances fail, they go down. Not so with Joseph! He was consistent. His story encourages us to do as another has admonished:

> *To talk with God, no breath is lost;*
> > *Talk on.*
> *To walk with God, no strength is lost;*
> > *Walk on.*
> *To wait on God, no time is lost;*
> > *Wait on.*

Whisked away from prison, quickly shaven and cleaned, Joseph now stood before ancient civilization's greatest monarch. Amidst the luxury of the royal court, Joseph's prison pallor was noticeable but he stood with head erect. He knew that he was there, not in the power of Pharaoh but under the authority of God.

Joseph now faces the greatest challenge of his life. Not only is he given an audience with Pharaoh himself; he is in a position of being able to help Pharaoh in a way no one else in the kingdom could. Will he be sufficient for the challenge? Already we are confident that he will be. We remember his own dreams; we recall his faithfulness to God both in the palace and in prison; we are aware of his accurate interpretation of the dreams of the cupbearer and the baker; but above all else, we know something very special about Joseph—the Lord was with him!

Joseph did not have time to think or to design elaborate plans—he had time only to act. Facing a crisis, with no time for preparation or pretense, Joseph would pass the test—not in his own power, but in the power of the Lord. God had been preparing him for thirteen years. All along Joseph had believed that God was faithful. But now he would see the expression of God's faithfulness as never before. God's time had come, and His man, Joseph, was ready.

When your big opportunity comes, will you be ready to meet it? To the degree that you have been faithful in the little things along the way, you will be ready for the opportunity of great moment. You will fail unless the Lord is with you as He was with Joseph.

When Pharaoh said that he had heard that Joseph could interpret dreams, Joseph humbly replied, "It is not in me: God shall give Pharaoh an answer of peace" (Genesis 41:16). His reply revealed both meekness and faith.

In Joseph's time Egypt was the center of learning and culture, but the people were idol worshipers. Now God showed Pharaoh that all human resources and wisdom are powerless and worthless apart from Him. World leaders today would be so wise if they would acknowledge their need of God's widsom.

Joseph's formula for success was: I

cannot, but God can. This is ours also: "I can do all things through Christ which strengtheneth me" (Philippians 4:13). God has chosen to do His marvelous work through the human vessel. It is true that "without God we cannot, and without us God will not." We are challenged to be His available channels by Charles Spurgeon's exhortation: "Rest no longer satisfied with thy dwarfish attainments, aspire to a higher, nobler, fuller life. Upward to heaven, near to God."

Joseph listened to Pharaoh recount his strange dreams (Genesis 41:17-24). Then he responded immediately with unusual clearness in interpreting the dreams. "The dream of Pharaoh is one: God hath shewed Pharaoh what he is about to do" (Genesis 41:25). Joseph first indicated that both the dreams, one bearing on the pastoral and the other on the agricultural life of Egypt, were predictive of the same thing. And he indicated that the dreams were a revelation of God's future action.

Pharaoh's dreams reflect to us the sovereignty of God in world events. His dreams were given to him by God. The timing of the dreams was according to God's schedule. The meaning of the dreams was God's plan. And the outcome would serve His sovereign purpose. Indeed, "The king's heart is in the hand of the Lord, as the rivers of water: he turneth it whithersoever He will" (Proverbs 21:1). The sovereignty of God in human events was underlined by Ben Franklin, one of America's founding fathers. In the beginning of the contest of the American Colonies with Great Britain he admonished the people to pray, and declared: "I have lived a long time, sir, and the longer I live the more convincing proof I see of this truth—that God governs in the affairs of men. And if a sparrow cannot fall to the ground without His notice, is it possible that an empire can rise without His aid?"

Against the backdrop of the perplexity of the Egyptian wise men, the inspired wisdom of Joseph appeared even more remarkable as he continued to interpret Pharaoh's dreams. He revealed that the dreams foretold seven years of plenty to be followed by seven years of devastating famine. The first seven years would produce bountiful harvests; the next seven years would bring want, suffering and death.

When Joseph interpreted the fatfleshed and leanfleshed cows in Pharaoh's dreams as omens of plenty and famine, the king was awed. It made sense. Egypt depended on the great Nile River to provide heaven-sent irrigation each year. It was the giver of life and refreshment to the ground. Hathor was the name of an Egyptian goddess reputed to be guised as a cow. Sacred bulls munched in sacred stalls amid mooing harems.

Joseph explained further the reason why the dream was given in two forms: "... it is because the thing is established by God, and God will shortly bring it to pass" (Genesis 41:32). The doubling of the dreams signified the certainty and the nearness of the divine purpose revealed. In giving two dreams God solidified the revelation by "two witnesses." The validation of two witnesses is recognized in both the Old Testament (Deuteronomy

19:15) and the New (Matthew 18:16).

Beyond the interpretation Joseph offered Pharaoh some sound managerial advice: "Now therefore let Pharaoh look out a man discreet and wise, and set him over the land of Egypt. Let Pharaoh do this, and let him appoint officers over the land, and take up the fifth part of the land of Egypt in the seven plenteous years. And let them gather all the food of those good years that come, and lay up corn under the hand of Pharaoh, and let them keep food in the cities. And that food shall be for store to the land against the seven years of famine, which shall be in the land of Egypt; that the land perish not through the famine" (Genesis 41:33-36). Not only did Joseph prove able to explain God's message, but he came up with a clear-cut plan of action. Without loss of time a leader of superior ability must be found to supervise agricultural production, store tremendous portions of grain, and later distribute the accumulated resources.

Once again, dreams played an important part in Joseph's life. Three sets of dreams were a vital part of his career. The middle pair of providential dreams (Genesis 40:5-7) proved to be the means for involving Joseph in the third pair (41:9-11); and this last pair served to exalt Joseph to the position of fulfilling the first pair (37:5-9).

Joseph's hour of triumph has come. He now is directed by His Lord in a great leap. He is moved from prison to palace in one day. All the dark trials of his past have prepared him for this day. He handled adversity well. How will he handle a new kind of test—the test of prosperity?

So pleased was Pharaoh with Joseph's wisdom in interpreting the dreams, and his reasonable and comprehensive plan, that he looked no further for a man to take the responsibility of the office of chief administrator. Pharaoh saw standing before him a young man noble in appearance, bright with intelligence, and calm with God's peace. "Can we find such a one as this is, a man in whom the Spirit of God is?" (Genesis 41:38), he exclaimed. Pharaoh immediately appointed Joseph to regulate the collection and distribution of food during the coming years.

God's sovereignty in bringing Joseph into power was emphasized years later by Stephen (Acts 7:9,10):

And the patriarchs, moved with envy, sold Joseph into Egypt: but God was with him, and delivered him out of all his afflictions, and gave him favour and wisdom in the sight of Pharaoh, king of Egypt; and he made him governor over Egypt and all his house.

The secret of Joseph's success was inferred by Pharaoh when he recognized Joseph as a man in whom a divine spirit abode. I am reminded of the evangelist Dwight L. Moody, who had great power with God and man in his generation. A group of men in Philadelphia were discussing the possibility of inviting him to preach in their city. After hearing so much about the evangelist, one man asked impatiently, "Does

Moody have a monopoly on the Holy Spirit?" "No," one of the men replied, "but the Holy Spirit has a monopoly on Moody."

Joseph was thirty years old when he was appointed as viceroy of Pharaoh's domain. Having been seventeen when he came to Egypt he probably spent ten years in Potiphar's house and three years in prison. In God's providence he was exalted from prisoner to prince. As the grand vizier or prime minister of Egypt he had command over the entire kingdom next to Pharaoh.

Pharaoh invested Joseph with the insignia of office and paraded him before the people (Genesis 41:42,43). The giving of gifts to a man being inducted into office was an Egyptian custom. Pharaoh's signet ring was placed on Joseph's hand as a badge of authority empowering him to issue official edicts.

A special official preceded Joseph's chariot and called out to the people "*Ab rek!*" ("Bow the knee"). The signal did not refer to prostration but probably meant "Pay attention!" and made clear to everyone that an outstanding man of ability and authority was passing by. Some interpret the signal also to mean that Pharaoh was proclaiming Joseph naturalized in order to remove any dislike that the people might have for him as a foreigner.

Pharaoh did everything he could to show how completely he desired to make Joseph feel at home in Egypt. He gave him an Egyptian name, Zaphenath-paneh, which means *the supporter of life* or *the food of the living*.

Pharaoh also gave to Joseph an Egyptian lady of high rank for his wife: " ... he gave him to wife Asenath the daughter of Potipherah priest of On" (Genesis 41:45). Joseph's naturalization was completed by this alliance with an Egyptian family of high distinction. On was later given the name Heliopolis, which is Greek for "city of the sun." Near modern Cairo, this city was the center for the worship of the sun god Ra. Some accuse Joseph, at this point, of marrying outside God's will for His chosen people. Others believe that the wife may have been a worshiper of the true God:

> *On being founded by an Arab colony, Poti-phereh, like Jethro, Priest of Midian, might be a worshiper of the true God; and thus Joseph, a pious man, will be freed from the charge of marrying an idolatress for worldly ends.* [1]

In any case, Joseph remained true to Jehovah.

Pharaoh could not change Joseph's heart, though he changed his name. An old expression is, "You can take the boy out of the country, but you can't take the country out of the boy." Of Joseph we may say: They could put the boy in Egypt, but they couldn't put Egypt in the boy! Joseph did well in sorting out the difference between his faith and his culture.

Joseph exercised great wisdom as an economist. He immediately "went throughout all the land of Egypt" (Genesis 41:46) to survey the country to determine the site and size of the storehouses that would be needed. In his countrywide trip, he no doubt made certain also that every part of the land suitable for cultivation would be planted with grain.

The gathering of grain began, and throughout the seven bountiful years the food was stored in the cities (Genesis 41:48). Such an abundance of grain was stored that all the granaries were full to overflowing and no one could keep track of the amount (verse 49).

Joseph exacted in the years of plenty a tax of one-fifth of the produce of the land. Though taking a fifth part of the crop involved a double tithe, it was no hardship on the people when the harvest was so plentiful. Had the surplus crop not been gathered, it might largely have been wasted by careless management. Through Joseph's orderly administration the surplus grain was stored in preparation for the famine.

Before the years of famine came, Asenath bore Joseph two sons. Joseph stamped out a permanent affirmation of his faith in the naming of his two sons. He gave to both Hebrew, not Egyptian, names. "And Joseph called the name of the firstborn Manasseh; For God, said he, hath made me forget all my toil, and all my father's house. And the name of the second called he Ephraim: For God hath caused me to be fruitful in the land of my affliction" (Genesis 41:51,52). Those two names, "forgetting" and "fruitful," capsulize the testimony of Joseph. Also, they indicate the two outstanding needs of every believer in relation to life's distressful experiences—

forgetting past suffering and fruitfulness in present service.

The name of the first son, "forgetting," indicates Joseph's happiness. God helped him to forget his past pains. Evidently, Joseph's forgetting included forgiveness. During his years of suffering Joseph was taught by God how to forgive his brothers for their terrible deed. When he meets them later, we witness his forgiveness.

Clara Barton, the founder of the American Red Cross, devoted her life to the good of humanity. Her carrying supplies to soldiers and nursing wounded men earned her the title "Angel of the Battlefield." A friend once expressed surprise that Clara did not seem to remember an unkindness that had been done to her some time before. Her reply was, "No, I distinctly remember forgetting it."

The name of Joseph's second son, "doubly fruitful," shows his prosperity. In his prosperity, Joseph did not forget God. He was not like the father who was asked by his little girl, "Daddy, is God dead?" as he tucked her in bed with a good night kiss. "No, dear. Why do you ask?" "Because I never hear you talking to Him anymore," she said. In Joseph's peak of prosperity he did not have a famine of faith.

The seven fat years ended and phase two of Joseph's prophecy began. Dearth swept over the land like a duststorm. Where fields had stood thick with shocks of corn, where reapers had pealed out songs of gladness, and where well-laden wagons had routed the turf with heavy wheel marks, there now was desolation. The sheaves were very few, the grain poor and blighted. Famine ruled, not only in Egypt but in the contiguous lands of Canaan, Syria, and Arabia. It "was over all the face of the earth" (Genesis 41:56). When the famine struck, Joseph "opened all the storehouses" to buyers, first from Egypt and then from all the other nations.

Perhaps Joseph's exaltation was his greatest test. Would he be able to accept success and still keep his heart right with God? I have noticed that to the degree a person acknowledges God in the "down" periods of his life, he will acknowledge Him in the "up" periods. After his rise to power Joseph was most careful to continue waiting before God. He resisted the natural temptation of pride with the same thoroughness as he had resisted the temptation of passion.

[1] R. Jamieson, A. R. Faussett, D. Brown, *A Commentary Critical and Explanatory on the Old and New Testaments* (Grand Rapids: Zondervan Publishing House, n.d.), p. 42.

9
When Testing Delays You

Two years into the famine in Canaan, Jacob and his family were feeling the shortage of grain. Hearing of the availability of grain in Egypt, Judah sent his ten oldest sons to buy food there, but he kept young Benjamin at home. The story that follows is a moving account of Joseph's testing and eventual reunion with his brothers.

When the ten brothers appeared before Joseph, he recognized them but they did not suspect his identity. Standing before them as the mightiest figure in Egypt, Joseph was disguised not only by physical changes but by his language, dress, and official bearing.

Rather than declare his identity, Joseph waited. His announcement of his identity would not be quick and impulsive as was his youthful announcement of his dreams. Why did he withhold his identity for so long? He was to determine whether their hearts and minds had undergone an entire change from the perfidious envy that had prompted them to sell him into slavery.

As the brothers bowed before Joseph he "remembered the dreams which he dreamed of them" (Genesis 42:9). The brothers were unaware that they were fulfilling the dreams that they had gone to desperate lengths to defeat. When they presented their request to Joseph, he curtly rebuffed them. To test them he used for his excuse the accusation that they were spies. "Ye are spies; Hereby ye shall be proved [tested]" (Genesis 42:14,15). Apparently Joseph wondered: "Are my brothers still the same, or have they learned their lesson and changed?"

Joseph's visitors denied that they were spies, and said, "Thy servants are twelve brethren, the sons of one man in the land of Canaan; and behold, the youngest is this day with our father and one is not" (Genesis 42:13). We can feel the catch of Joseph's heart as he heard of his father and his younger brother.

Acting as God's representative, Joseph followed a carefully laid plan for bringing his brothers to repentance. Probably he was bursting with the desire to disclose himself to his brothers, but he realized he dare not do this and spoil God's program. Joseph's treatment of his brothers bore a strange mixture of harshness and magnanimity. He skillfully played alternately on their fears and their hopes. His harshness was only a part of his disguise. Behind the harshness lay complete and generous forgiveness of the wrong done to him and a deep understanding of God's control of human destiny.

The tenderness behind Joseph's dealings with his brothers is the characteristic of all of God's allotments in our lives. God is abundant in goodness and mercy. It is God's infinite kindness that hedges our way with thorns. "For whom the Lord loveth he chasteneth, and scourgeth every son whom he receiveth" (Hebrews 12:6).

Joseph seized on the reference to the youngest brother as a test of the brothers' honesty. The acid test that he secretly saw was to determine whether the brothers would treat their youngest brother the same way they had treated Joseph. To get Benjamin to Egypt, Joseph at first said that one person should go for him while the others stayed. The brothers then were placed in prison for three days. There they had time to think and to talk about the reason for their desperate situation.

At the end of the imprisonment Joseph revised his plan:

This do, and live; for I fear God: if ye be true men, let one of your brethren be bound in the house of your prison: Go ye, carry corn for the famine of your houses: But bring your youngest brother unto me; so shall your words be verified, and ye shall not die (Genesis 42:18-20).

When Joseph demanded that the brother bring Benjamin back to Egypt he overheard them confessing their ill-fortune to be the result of their own sin:

> *We are verily guilty concerning our brother, in that we saw the anguish of his soul, when he besought us, and we would not hear; therefore is this distress come upon us (Genesis 42:21).*

They were deeply reproached with their past sins of hateful cruelty to their brother. It all flashed before them. Reuben underlined their guilt by reminding them: "Spake I not unto you, saying, Do not sin against the child; and ye would not hear? therefore, behold, also his blood is required" (Genesis 42:22).

Till now, Joseph did not know of Reuben's attempt to save him. They did not realize that he could understand them, since he had spoken to them through an interpreter, and now there was no interpreter around.

Joseph was deeply touched as he heard his brothers' reasoning, and "he turned himself about from them, and wept" (Genesis 42:24). He had to find a private place where he could relieve his full heart by a burst of tears. This is the first record of Joseph weeping. Evidently he wept more over relationships than over his own adversities. He had a heart of tender love. Seven times we read that he wept (see also Genesis 43:30; 45:2,14,15; 46:29; and 50:1).

Returning to his brothers, Joseph "took from them Simeon, and bound him before their eyes" (Genesis 42:24). He kept Simeon as a hostage to insure their return with Benjamin and sent the others back to their father with the grain they had come to buy.

Joseph sent them on their way with more than they realized! He "commanded to fill their sacks with corn, and to restore every man's money into his sack, and to give them provision for the way" (Genesis 42:25). After traveling some hours, they stopped for the night. As one of the brothers fed his donkey, he discovered money tied up in a bundle in the mouth of his sack. He was struck with fear, and so were his brothers when he told them. "And their hearts failed them, and they were afraid, saying one to another, What is this that God hath done unto us?" (Genesis 42:28). But worse than this, when they reached home and emptied their sacks, they and Jacob were mystified to find every man's money in his sack.

The sons recounted to Jacob the events of their trip and told him of the Egyptian's demand that they bring Benjamin with them on their next trip. Jacob was distressed over Simeon and refused to allow Benjamin to go. He exclaimed "Me have ye bereaved of my children: Joseph is not, and Simeon is not, and ye will take Benjamin away: all these things are against me" (Genesis 42:36).

Under the pressure of trials Jacob saw things only from the human perspective, and concluded: "... all these things are against me." The immediate circumstances were all that Jacob could see and in them he saw no hope whatever. Rather than all things being against Jacob, actually all things were working together for his good. This is the promise that God had made to every one of His children: "And we know that all things work together for good to them that love God, to them who are the called according to his purpose" (Romans 8:28).

Would you enjoy eating a few handfuls of flour? Would a spoonful of spices be more appetizing? How about a cup of shortening? Probably none of these things appeal to your appetite. None of these items are palatable by themselves, but when my wife mixes these ingredients together to make a delightful cake the story is different. Life's experiences are similar. Not all are "good." In fact some of the experiences God allows cannot be described as anything but bad. Yet God moves in a beautiful way to cause all things to work together for good.

Benjamin had taken the place of Joseph in his father's heart. Jacob would not permit him to go with the brothers to Egypt for fear of losing him. Reuben pledged to his father that he would be security for Benjamin: "Slay my two sons to death, if I bring him not to thee; deliver him into my hand, and I will bring him to thee again" (Genesis 42:37).

Jacob could not postpone the inevitable decision. When the supply of grain was again nearly exhausted, he requested that his nine sons make a second trip to Egypt for food. Judah stepped forward with a most earnest plea for his father to let Benjamin go. He pledged his own life to guarantee the safe return of the youngest son: "I will be surety for him; of my hand shalt thou require him: if I bring him not unto thee, and set him before thee, then let me bear the blame before you for ever" (Genesis 43:9). Reluctantly Jacob at last consented to entrust the lad to Judah's care.

Before sending his sons on another trip to Egypt Jacob prayed that God Almighty ('El Shaddai) would keep them and supply every need (Genesis 43:14). This is the Name by which Isaac blessed Jacob (Genesis 28:3) and the Name whereby God identified Himself when He appeared to Jacob and blessed him (Genesis 35:11). Its root, the Hebrew word for "breast," *Shaddai* means *all-sufficient nourisher* or *bountiful provider*. This name assures us that God is "more than enough" in our times of need.

Joseph probably saw his brothers first from a distance as they appeared before his steward at the entrance of his palace. Seeing that Benjamin was with them, Joseph ordered the preparation of a feast. The brothers were brought into the palace to prepare themselves for the dinner.

While the brothers were waiting at the palace they reasoned concerning the purpose of the feast and concluded:

Because of the money that was returned in our sacks at the first time are we brought in; that he may seek occasion against us, and fall upon us, and take us for bondmen, and our asses (Genesis 43:18).

Convinced that they should be the first to mention the money if they were to prove their innocence, the brothers spoke about it to the steward at the entrance to the house. The steward told them not to worry about it and assured them that God had given them the money: "Fear not: your God, and the God of your father, hath given you treasure in your sacks; I had your money" (Genesis 43:23).

Joseph released Simeon to join his brothers for the banquet. Upon meeting the brothers Joseph inquired about the health of their father. When he greeted Benjamin he was so stirred with love for him that he made a hasty exit to his bedroom to weep. He knew that he still should not reveal himself because God's program was not yet completed. Joseph was well trained to wait for God's time.

The record of Joseph's emotions at this time arouses tremendous pathos in the reader. I remember once when Rose and I took turns reading a portion of Genesis each day during our prayer time. When I stopped reading at the end of chapter 42 I waited for Rose to close her Bible as I closed mine. But with curiosity she continued to scan the next chapter silently. Engrossed in her curious pursuit, she was unaware that I sat watching her. When I noticed tears welling up in her eyes I checked chapter 43 to discover the reason. And I knew that she had come to the point of Joseph's meeting with his young brother Benjamin:

And he lifted up his eyes, and saw his brother Benjamin, his mother's son, and said, Is this your younger brother, of whom you spake unto me? And he said, May God be gracious to you, my son.... And Joseph made haste; for his bowels did yearn upon his brother: and he sought where to weep; and he entered into his chamber, and wept there" (Genesis 43:29,30).

For the banquet one table was set for Joseph, another for the eleven brothers, a third for the Egyptians. Probably the Egyptians considered that the presence of foreigners at their table defiled their food. The brothers were amazed when they realized that they were seated in the order of their ages, from the oldest to the youngest. How would a stranger know their ages? A second surprise at the feast bewildered them: the special favor shown to Benjamin. When portions of food were brought from Joseph's table to his brothers, Benjamin was given five times as much as any of the others.

Why did Joseph give Benjamin portions five times larger than those given to the others? Because Benjamin was favored by his father, the brothers' feeling toward him could be the same as it had been toward Joseph. Joseph now showed favor to Benjamin in order to watch the brothers' reaction. While favor was shown to Benjamin at Joseph's meal, any envy and hatred that the brothers might have for him would manifest itself in their reaction. Evidently they passed the test. Joseph saw a remarkable change in them as "they drank, and were merry with him" (Genesis 43:34). Without anxiety and care the brothers feasted and drank well in an occasion they could not forget. By the end of the meal Joseph knew them much better and saw that they had changed.

Joseph had one final test that was calculated to reveal a clear picture of his brothers' inner hearts. When at last the brothers were ready to depart for home, Joseph's steward was ordered to enclose their money in each sack as before and to add a richly ornamented silver cup, a royal treasure, to Benjamin's sack. A short distance from the city the steward overtook the Israelites and accused them of stealing the silver cup. The brothers felt entirely guiltless, unaware of what Joseph had done. They readily agreed to a search of the bags, declaring: "With whomsoever of thy servants it be found, both let him die, and we also will be my lord's bondmen" (Genesis 44:9). The steward pronounced a lighter penalty: "He with whom it is found shall be my servant, and the rest of you shall be blameless" (Genesis 44:10).

The search began with the oldest son. When the very last sack was emptied, all stood breathless as the sharp rattle of metal struck their ears and the gleam of silver dazzled their eyes. Rending their clothes, they sadly put their sacks back on the beasts and rode back to the city, not knowing what punishment awaited them.

In utter dismay, the brothers were returned to the governor. They fell at his feet with bewildered despair. Judah spoke for the group in reply to Joseph's accusations. Whether they were guilty of stealing the goblet or not, Judah realized that they had committed a terrible sin in selling their brother into slavery. He frankly confessed his own sins and the sins of his brothers:

What shall we say unto my lord? what

*shall we speak? or how shall we clear
ourselves? God hath found out the
iniquity of thy servants: behold, we are
my lord's slaves, both we, and he also
with whom the cup is found (Genesis
44:16).*

Joseph rejected this plea and lifted the
situation to an agony of tension when he
demanded that Benjamin should remain as
his slave while the others returned to their
home.

While his brothers continued kneeling
before Joseph in mute grief, Judah came
closer to him with a tender and earnest plea
for Benjamin. In admiration of Judah's plea,
Martin Luther said: "What would I not give to
be able to pray before the Lord as Judah here
interceded for Benjamin, for it is a perfect
model of prayer, nay, of the strong feeling that
must underlie all prayer."

With beautiful simplicity Judah reviewed
the story of their encounters with the
governor. He spoke of Jacob's loss of one
son and his reluctance to part with Benjamin,
overcome only by the harsh necessity of
hunger. He insisted that their return without
the lad would be the death-stroke to their
aged father. His words concerning the grief of
his father are deeply touching:

*Now therefore when I come to thy ser-
vant my father, and the lad is not with us;
seeing his life is bound up in the lad's
life; it shall come to pass, when he seeth
that the lad is not with us, that he will
die: and thy servants shall bring down the*

*gray hairs of thy servant our father with
sorrow to the grave (Genesis 44:30-32).*

Judah's final appeal was a heroic offer to
become a bondsman in his brother's place for
the sake of their aged father. The spirit of
self-sacrifice once so foreign to Judah now
shone forth with rare beauty.

*Now therefore I pray thee, let thy servant
abide instead of the lad a bondman to
my lord; and let the lad go up with his
brethren. For how shall I go up to my
father, and the lad be not with me? lest
peradventure I see the evil that shall
come on my father? (Genesis 44:33,34).*

Have you seen what Joseph was doing in
his well-thought, deep-laid, and closely-
connected plan? He actually set up circumstances that duplicated the situation in
which he was betrayed by his brothers. He
tested the honesty and repentance of his
brothers. He ordered to Egypt Jacob's
favorite son, Benjamin. He tried the brothers
at the table to determine whether they
cherished the same bitter feelings against
Benjamin that had governed their conduct
toward Joseph. He put them in that old
situation of appearing before Jacob without
one brother to determine whether they would
betray a favored son to save themselves. He
ran the test to the very end. Judah's final plea
was the capstone evidence of changed
brothers and was more than Joseph could
bear.

10
When Reconciliation
Can't Hold Back

Joseph's heart was too full to bear Judah's earnest plea. The feelings that had been swelling in his breast were about to burst forth. The test was completed! No longer could he act the stranger to his brothers.

Eleven brothers received the greatest alarm of their lives when the Egyptian governor shouted for everyone else to leave the room. His meeting with his brothers was not for strangers to see. It was a delicate moment that naturally would reveal their past sin. Joseph would not expose his brothers' sin to a group of onlookers. Also this was an intimate time of reunion that must be private.

The brothers stood astonished as Joseph turned back to them and wept so loudly that he could be heard all over the palace. His pent-up emotions were released at last! "He wept aloud" (Genesis 45:2), literally *he gave forth himself in weeping.*

In a scene of inimitable power and tenderness Joseph "made himself known unto his brethren." His sudden announcement shocked them: "I am Joseph; doth my father yet live?" (Genesis 45:3). So startled and confused were they that they were speechless. He called them closer and told them again, "I am Joseph your brother, whom ye sold into Egypt" (Genesis 45:4).

Seeing their evident distress, Joseph did not let his brothers speak until he quickly took from their shoulders the burden of blame: "Now therefore be not grieved nor angry with yourselves, that ye sold me hither: for God did send me before you to preserve life" (Genesis 45:5). The divine plot of the past fifteen years' scenario was clear to him. Repeatedly he insisted that God had willed it as a means of preserving Israel:

And God sent me before you to preserve you a posterity in the earth, and to save your lives by a great deliverance. So now, it was not you that sent me hither, but God: and He has made me a father to Pharaoh, and lord of all his house, and a ruler throughout all the land of Egypt (Genesis 45:7,8).

Joseph had learned not to blame his circumstances on people but to see God as the controller of his life. God, not man, orders our circumstances. Joseph endeavored to comfort his brothers by showing them how all had turned out for the best, how God had brought good out of evil and had caused sin to be the occasion of deliverance and blessing to them all.

Joseph completely forgave his brothers. As far as he was concerned their evil against him would never be brought up again. That is like our heavenly Father's forgiveness! How blessed we are to be forgiven by Him on the basis of the substitutionary death of our Savior. A bumper sticker stated it well: "I'm not perfect—just forgiven!" Being a *forgiven* person makes the Christian *forgiving*! Paul put it this way: "And be ye kind one to another, tenderhearted, forgiving one another, even as God for Christ's sake hath forgiven you" (Ephesians 4:32).

Having assured his brothers of his forgiveness, Joseph urged them to go quickly to their father and to bring the entire family into Egypt that he might be with them and care for them. "And thou shalt dwell in the land of Goshen; and thou shalt be near unto me, thou, and thy children, and thy children's children, and thy flocks, and thy herds, and all that thou hast" (Genesis 45:10).

Aware that they still could not believe what was happening, Joseph said: "And, behold, your eyes see, and the eyes of my brother Benjamin see, that it is my mouth that speaketh unto you" (Genesis 45:12).

Probably not until the brothers felt Joseph's hug pressing them against his heart and his hot tears falling on their cheeks could they truly believe that it was he. "And he fell upon his brother Benjamin's neck, and wept; and Benjamin wept on his neck. Moreover he kissed all his brethren, and wept upon them:

and after that his brethren talked with him" (Genesis 45:14,15).

There was no small stir in Pharaoh's palace that day! Everyone was pleased to know of Joseph's happy reunion. Pharaoh commanded that the brothers take treasures to the aged patriarch Jacob and bring him and all his household back to Egypt. Wagons were provided for carrying all their possessions in the move. The wagons were filled with grain, presents, and supplies of all kinds. The eleven brothers set forth, thrilled with the news they were taking to their aged father.

To Jacob the news was too good to be true. "Jacob's heart fainted, for he believed them not" (Genesis 45:26). It took a long time of their telling the whole story and showing their father the wagons sent by Joseph before Jacob's numb spirit revived and he exclaimed, "It is enough; is my son Joseph yet alive: I will go and see him before I die" (Genesis 45:28). With all his people and possessions, Jacob left for Egypt on a day of comfort and rejoicing for one who had seen much grief.

From Hebron Jacob came to Beersheba, where in a night vision God spoke to him encouraging him in his move and assuring him of uncounted blessings. It appears that Jacob deferred his sacrifice till he reached the spot at Beersheba where God's covenant had been consecrated to his father, Isaac, and grandfather, Abraham. This was to be Jacob's last journey, and he began it with God. He approached God through a sacrifice and God responded to him. Consideration of God's warning to Abraham of a sojourn in a foreign land (Genesis 15:13-15) made Jacob's departure from Canaan a challenge to the depths of his faith in the covenant's future. At the patriarchal altar site on the borders of the land he received a virtual renewal of the covenant and an assurance of its blessings.

In this last in the series of special revelations that marked his pilgrim life, Jacob was reassured that the land of Canaan would be given to him and his descendants. Though Jacob now was leaving Canaan with all his family, God confirmed His promise and revealed to Jacob His plan for ultimately bringing his seed back to the promised land. God's promise included the following elements: *peace*, "Fear not to go down into Egypt"; *purpose*, "for I will there make of thee a great nation"; *presence*, "I will go down with thee into Egypt"; *power*, "and I will also surely bring thee up again"; and *protection*, "And Joseph shall put his hands upon thine eyes" (Genesis 46:3,4). The promise that Joseph would close Jacob's eyes was a prophecy that Jacob's last rites would be performed by his own illustrious son.

Encouraged by the heavenly vision, Jacob proceeded on the long journey. He chose Judah to go in advance of the company to meet Joseph and complete the arrangements for their entrance into Goshen. Jacob and his caravan of sixty-six persons (Jacob, Joseph, and Joseph's two sons make the total of seventy referred to in Genesis 46:27), with their wives and servants, entered the land of Goshen.

Still the same affectionate son, Joseph

was overjoyed to be reunited with his father. He came out in his chariot to meet Jacob at Goshen. Then he fell on Jacob's neck and wept a long time. "And Israel [Jacob] said unto Joseph, Now let me die, since I have seen thy face, because thou art yet alive" (Genesis 46:30). Jacob's happiness was at its height and life could have no higher charms for him; he would have been ready now to die in peace. Both father and son were unable to speak for a long time, but only embrace and weep. Never was there a more tender meeting of two hearts than that of Joseph and his aged father on the plain.

Joseph already had planned for his family to settle in Goshen, but he knew that Pharaoh must sanction such a move. Five brothers were chosen by Joseph to represent the family before Pharaoh. Joseph instructed them to tell Pharaoh that they were shepherds who had come to sojourn in the land because the famine was severe in Canaan. They were told to request permission to settle in Goshen, since Joseph knew that this would provide secluded security for his people. Pharaoh not only granted their request but asked Joseph to appoint some of the best men to places of responsibility among his cattlemen.

The climax of the occasion was Joseph's presentation of his aged father to Pharaoh, who received Jacob with the courtesy of an Eastern monarch. He respected the sight of age that far exceeded the ordinary term of life in Egypt. When Pharaoh asked Jacob his age, Jacob said that his 130 years were "few" compared to that of his fathers, and said they had been unpleasant (Genesis 47:9). Jacob's life had been full of trouble, sin, and sorrow. But now he was to see the blessing of God. Having led him through his stormy pilgrim days, God now brought Jacob to a quiet home near his beloved son where he should spend the remainder of his days on earth in peace.

Though a foreigner and a recipient of Pharaoh's assistance, Jacob stood before the great ruler with dignity. In the consciousness that he was the representative of the Almighty, "Jacob blessed Pharaoh" (Genesis 47:10). Knowing that he held a sublime position in God's program, he spoke the holy blessing upon Pharaoh.

The child of God always may stand with dignity as the representative of the Almighty Father, even before an earthly ruler. We represent the Savior wherever we go.

Joseph had known that his family would be allowed to "dwell in the land of Goshen; for every shepherd is an abomination unto the Egyptians" (Genesis 46:34). In times of famine nomads from Palestine were known to have been allowed pasturage in the Eastern Delta. The Egyptian dislike of nomadic shepherds, like that of most settled people for wandering gypsies, served to keep the family of Israel as an isolated unit to maintain identity. Egyptian records show that shepherds were considered the lowest class or caste because of their nomadic habits. Some believe that the Egyptian dislike of the shepherd occupation stemmed from their past history when their land was overrun by a rough race of shepherd kings who treated the

Egyptians very cruelly.

Pharaoh ordered that the Hebrew family be located in "Rameses." This region called "Goshen" only in the Bible, was a valley that stretched for thirty-five miles from the Nile to Lake Timsah in the Eastern Delta. Rendered fertile by a canal, it was the best natural meadowland in Egypt. Joseph's people were given an abundance of supplies for the remaining years of famine. Dwelling nearby in Avaris, Joseph remained close to his father for the remainder of Jacob's days, providing lavish care and love for him. Joseph's people stayed on in the Delta after the lean years for nearly 400 years. Cuneiform and Egyptian texts of these times refer to an apparently alien people called *Habiru*.

God brought Israel to Egypt at this time in her history for the purposes of preservation, multiplication, and cultivation. The nation was to be preserved from not only the temporary threat of extinction by the famine but also the more dangerous threat of being absorbed into the Canaanite culture. By her removal to Egypt Israel was kept apart from the demoralizing influence of Canaan whose sin would increase so greatly that it would be judged by God, as revealed years earlier to Abraham (Genesis 15:13-16). Israel's confinement in Goshen would preserve her also against mixed marriages that would debilitate the Hebrew race.

Goshen afforded ample room for Israel to increase. The nation presently was a mere handful of people. Begun in Abraham, it now numbered seventy (Genesis 46:27). In Egypt God would multiply and solidify the nation:

"And Israel dwelt in the land of Egypt, in the country of Goshen; and they had possessions therein, and grew, and multiplied exceedingly" (Genesis 47:27). Four hundred years later Israel would be a large nation ready for the exodus.

In Egypt, Israel's identity as God's chosen people would be established. There she would be trained and cultivated by the pressure of future bondage. As Joseph was matured through his adversities in Egypt, so would the nation of Israel be prepared by God through its future period of enslavement there. Joseph is important as the link between the *family* of Israel and the *nation* of Israel. Up to the time of Joseph the Israelites were a famlly. After Joseph's day they were a nation.

11
When Leadership Suits You

Joseph was one of the first administrators in Scripture. He was the ideal son, the ideal brother, the ideal servant, and the ideal administrator. In his relating to people and his managing the Egyptian economy we learn lessons relevant to positions of leadership that we are involved in today.

The famine conditions in Egypt grew worse and the people fell into dire need. From all over the realm people came to Joseph for aid. When their money was exhausted, they traded their cattle for grain (Genesis 47:17). The following year they offered their land and themselves to secure more food for their families:

When that year was ended, they came unto him the second year, and said unto him, "We will not hide it from my lord, how that our money is spent; my lord also hath our herds of cattle; there is not ought left in the sight of my lord, but our bodies, and our lands: Wherefore shall we die before thine eyes, both we and our land? buy us and our land for bread, and we and our land will be servants unto Pharaoh: and give us seed, that we may live, and not die, that the land be not desolate" (Genesis 47:18,19).

All the lands of the realm except the holdings of the priests became Pharaoh's property. As the proprietor of the land of Egypt, Pharaoh supplied the people with food until the famine was past. To manage the distribution conveniently, Joseph brought the people of each district into their nearest cities where the granaries were.

Seed was distributed to all the people to be sown in their fields, with the agreement that a fifth of the produce would be given to Pharaoh. Joseph's statement, "Here is seed for you, and ye shall sow the land" (Genesis 47:23), apparently indicates that the gift was not to be repeated. The seed enabled the people to begin a new era of productivity. Twenty percent of their crop each year thereafter was to be yielded to Pharaoh.

The people agreed to the drastic measures because of their respect for Joseph to whom they declared: "Thou hast saved our lives: let us find grace in the sight of my lord, and we will be Pharaoh's servants" (Genesis 47:25). The proposal came from the people themselves, and they were satisfied with the arrangement. They received nourishment for the duration of the famine, continued holding their lands as the king's tenants, and paid a double tithe as the only public burden.

Serving as Egypt's prime minister, Joseph provided the people's needs while he increased the king's greatness and glory by his wise management. He kept himself in the background and exalted only the king. Pharaoh had good reason to be satisfied as he became master of the lives and property of his subjects.

Though Pharaoh's reign as an absolute monarch was acceptable for a while, it could not be eternal. Ultimately a monarch, being imperfect, abuses and loses his power. But one day the perfect King, our Lord Jesus Christ, will rule the earth with the power of God: "And he shall judge the world in righteousness, he shall minister judgment to the people in uprightness" (Psalm 9:8). Then the world will know what a perfect absolute government is.

We are admonished in I Timothy 2:1-6 to pray for persons in positions of leadership in government. The immediate aim of prayer for our leaders should be peace and godliness. The ultimate and supreme goal of our prayer should be the salvation of lost persons and the spread of the gospel of Jesus Christ, who alone is able to meet the heart needs of mankind.

God used Joseph to provide economic stability for Egypt and dependent nations in a time of world famine. But that was only a temporal accomplishment. The ultimate goal of God was the preservation and preparation of His chosen people for the accomplishment of His Messianic objective.

The Christian has a responsibility not only to pray for his leaders, but to support political candidates who will lead the government righteously. God has revealed in His Word how groups of people should live together to promote peace, harmony, and justice. The best form of government is neither a monarch nor a democracy, but a theocracy. The Old Testament was written for a theocracy, the nation of Israel living under the divine control of God. There is no such theocracy today. The New Testament was written for the church in a pluralistic society. The Christian does not make an idol of his society or his political ideologies, but submits his politics to the risen Lord by weighing every political issue in the light of Scripture.

Biblical principles that have profound importance for our politics are the sacredness of human life, the family as a divinely-willed institution, religious and political freedom, preservation of peace, righteous social structure, personal integrity, just economic patterns, concern for the poor and oppressed, and stewardship of earth's resources. To the extent that secular societies live up to revealed standards they will enjoy peace and wholeness.

A political candidate is to be evaluated by his commitment to fundamental Biblical principles concerning society, his record in promoting programs consistent with Biblical principles, and his ability in leading others to pursue those principles. One should strive to support candidates most concerned about the whole range of principles listed above. God's standard for the earthly leader is indicated in Proverbs 16:12,13:

> *It is an abomination to kings to commit wickedness: for the throne is established by righteousness. Righteous lips are the delight of kings; and they love him that speaketh right.*

Joseph was a model leader. Consider seven key qualities of leadership that are seen in him:

1. *Calling.* Joseph had a sense of mission that defied human circumstances. Faithfulness to the call of God was the driving purpose of his life.

Frank Sinatra has been quoted as summing up his approach to life in this way: "I'm going to do as I please. I don't need anybody in the world. I did it all myself." Tragically, that is the creed of too many self-worshipers who ignore their Creator's claims upon their lives. Joseph was different.

Joseph had a dream and he endured the hardships of life through faith in his Lord until he saw that dream fulfilled. Though Satan intensified his attack upon him, Joseph persisted in whatever work God gave him to do, and he retained his sense of mission unto its amazing fulfillment. Nothing that he gained was handed to him on a silver platter; he matured through adversity.

2. *Conviction.* Joseph had an abiding faith in the Lord. Repeatedly we are reminded of his sense of dependence on God's guidance and help. His walk with God enabled him to maintain spiritual discipline. He had courage in the face of opposition, resistance at the

time of temptation, and steadfastness in fires of adversity.

Alexander F. Laidlaw, a Canadian outstanding in adult education, identifies two characteristics that all leaders have in common:

(1) They are deeply attached to an idea or a set of ideas. Great leaders are men of strong convictions. They believe in something very deeply. We may not admire what they stand for, but there can never be any doubt that they have firm beliefs. So, leadership starts in the mind of the leader—it has its foundation in ideas and a philosophy. Leaders are devoted to a cause.

(2) The leader is able in one way or another to transmit his ideas and convictions to others, and in such a way as to make others follow him. And ideas can be communicated in other ways besides speech—some leaders get their ideas across by the written word, by books. [1]

3. *Character.* People must feel in their leader a sense of solidity, honesty, and reliability. He must give evidence of having consistent motives and upright character.

Joseph was a man of personal integrity. He refused to sin against his master and against his Lord by giving in to Potiphar's wife. He faithfully fulfilled his duties whether in the palace or the prison. The mark of a righteous leader is that he is not driven by the desire for power. Joseph did not use his position under Pharaoh for personal gain, but he always served the king's best interests.

Joseph demonstrated that a believer does not have to compromise his standards in order to become a success. Joseph's faith touched every area of his daily life. No associate of his was left wondering about his relationship with God. He exemplified the commitment that Paul admonishes the Christian to have: "And whatsoever ye do in word or deed, do all in the name of the Lord Jesus, giving thanks to God and the Father by him" (Colossians 3:17).

4. *Commitment.* Joseph always acknowledged and honored God. The Lord was the motivating power in his life. To Potiphar's wife he insisted, "How then could I ... sin against God?" To his fellow prisoners he declared, "Do not interpretations belong to God?" To Pharaoh he affirmed, "God will give Pharaoh a favorable answer." In his prosperity he testified, "God has made me forget .... God has made me fruitful." To his brothers he maintained, "I fear God," and "It was not you who sent me here, but God."

One evening during the Civil War President Abraham Lincoln waited with some of his officials for news from the battlefront. The question was posed to him by one of the men, "Sir, do you believe that God is on our side?" Lincoln's wise reply was, "The question is not whether God is on our side but are we on God's side!" One cannot expect God to be committed to his cause unless his cause issues from the will of God.

5. *Confidence.* A leader must be an

optimist; he must believe that dreams can come true. He imagines what has to be done and believes that it will be done. He is absorbed not in complaining and criticizing but in thinking constructively and acting positively. Joseph's experiences as a slave and prisoner taught him to trust God. When finally his prison door was opened, he sprang forth with a confidence in God that defied all the magicians and wise men of Egypt. God was on his side, and he knew it. Not in humanistic self-confidence but in humble faith he declared, "It is not in me; God will give Pharaoh a favorable answer."

Decisiveness is a requirement of good leadership. Joseph did not wring his hands and wonder what could be done about the situation that was to come upon Egypt and the world. Exhibiting great vision and creative imagination he stepped forth with a plan and presented it in a manner that convinced Pharaoh. Then he set out to fulfill his vision.

Joseph had the assurance that characterizes successful Christian leaders. He was positive and confident. An old cavalry motto is, "When in doubt, gallop!" The activity of supposed leaders sometimes turns out to be the gallop of uncertainty. But Joseph's actions were motivated by a confident faith.

6. *Capability.* God commits to men the gifts necessary for the tasks to which He calls them. Joseph's capabilities were obvious early in his life. Potiphar saw "how the Lord caused all that he did to prosper in his hand," and he made him overseer of his entire household. In the round house prison Joseph was made the

supervisor. When he interpreted Pharaoh's dreams he immediately was appointed to be prime minister.

Joseph exercised foresight in executing the administrative task of planning. He knew how to invest in the future and proved this in his proposal that immediately followed his interpretation of Pharaoh's dreams. Joseph had vision, that quality that perceives and interprets facts and confidently launches a dynamic course of action. When Helen Keller, blind from birth, was asked what she considered to be the greatest tragedy that could befall a person, she instinctively responded, "To have sight but lack vision." To make careful plans and organize strategy for the work of God is not unspiritual, it is Scriptural.

Joseph was an enterprising person whose energy and initiative in handling Egypt's business commended him to all the nation. Someone has said that there are three kinds of people in the world: a few who make things happen, a relative majority who watch things happen, and an overwhelming group who do not have any idea what is happening. Joseph was one of the few who made things happen.

Joseph looked into the future, anticipated trends and events, and prepared accordingly. He was able to orient the forces of change toward desirable goals. He was an "MBO" man—he managed by objectives.

Peter Drucker, an authority on administration, has described an effective decision as "a systematic process with clearly defined elements and a distinct sequence of steps." [2] Weighed by these criteria Joseph's decisions for famine relief were marvelous. J. D. Arnold writes that the aim of decision making is to "select that course of action which is expected to yield the greatest return for the least commitment of expenditure of resources." [3] Follow Joseph's strategy and see how it yielded the greatest return!

Joseph was adept in the area of control, the guiding of people to assure effective action toward the attainment of objectives. He managed people well in the three positions that he held. He exercised good common sense. Piety and practicality are not mutually exclusive qualities of life. Joseph's shrewd strategy is seen in his preparation of his family for their meeting with Pharaoh. By bringing the needs of his people before Pharaoh, Joseph prevented the possibility that someone would accuse him of favoritism. When Pharaoh appointed land for the Israelites, no one else in the kingdom would thwart his plan.

Joseph was a motivator. As a catalyst or change-agent, he stimulated the development of character in others, evidenced in his testing of his brothers before he revealed to them his identity.

Organizational skill was exercised by Joseph in his early management positions and in his role as prime minister, in which he handled the entire population of Egypt. An intelligent leader knows how best to utilize the gifts of others and coordinate the specialized efforts of all units within his organization. The leader's ability to see the enterprise as a whole is emphasized by Ordway Tead: "The coordinative technique means ability to help formulate, transmit, interpret and supervise the working out of policies with people—with the members of the group from top to bottom." [4]

7. *Compassion.* Joseph was compassionate and tender toward others. Witness his sensitivity to the feelings of his two fellow prisoners as well as his kindheartedness toward his brothers. He was magnanimous in his treatment of men who had mistreated him. A good leader has a high degree of empathy, a kind of built-in thermostat responsive to the needs and wishes of others.

Joseph did not use his position to lord it over others. He was benevolent toward all. A worker in a Christian institution that we once visited sought Rose's counsel regarding her difficult working situation. "I never knew where I stood," she said, "I was always reprimanded but never commended. I unwittingly related to God the leadership that I saw, and thought of God in the same way that I thought of the Director. Consequently I became fearful of God. It was several weeks before I realized why I had become so knotted up inside." The leader had failed to serve others in his leadership.

A good leader is alert to the needs people have and sensitive to their attitudes in the face of crisis and decision. From my study of the subject I define leadership as service to a group through the influencing of its members toward self-fulfillment and group unity in the accomplishment of mutually desirable objectives. The leader who has sympathetic warmth, friendliness, and solicitude will be able to influence others.

[1] Alexander F. Laidlaw, "Leaders and Leadership" *Adult Leadership*, November, 1972, p. 171.

[2] Peter Drucker, *The Effective Executive*, New York, Harper and Row, 1967, p. 113.

[3] J. D. Arnold, *The Art of Decision Making*, New York: American Management Association, Inc., 1980, p. 59.

[4] Ordway Tead, *The Art of Leadership*, New York: McGraw-Hill Publishing Company, Inc., 1935, p. 118.

12
When Death Darkens Your Path

Jacob's last years of peace contrasted sharply with the tumultuous years that preceded his arrival in Egypt. As he had had Joseph for seventeen years before his son's disappearance, he spent an additional seventeen years with him after their reunion at Goshen. During this time Jacob's family acquired property in Goshen, were productive, and became very numerous (Genesis 47:27). Jacob lived to witness the beginning of the fulfillment of God's promise to Abraham that his seed would be like the stars of the sky.

After his troubled days of hard struggle Jacob had enjoyed a long and peaceful evening, but now the night was falling. His children soon would lose their father. As his death drew near, Jacob called for Joseph and made him promise to bury him in the family burial place in Canaan, the land promised to the seed of Abraham. Joseph lovingly set his dear father's mind at ease by a solemn oath to do so.

Receiving Joseph's promise Jacob "bowed himself upon the bed's head" (Genesis 47:31). The man whose heart once was bowed in grief was now bowed in worship. He had been an oppressed man. Engulfed in sorrow he had moved on under the revelation of an unrecognized love and unseen purpose. Now his tears were wiped away. The "frowning providence" had unveiled a "smiling face." The Most High had ruled in all Jacob's earthly affairs, and out of seeming tragedy He had brought glorious triumph.

What a wonderful God we have! His ways often are beyond our human scrutiny. But our faith patiently waits the unfolding of His purposes. The circumstances that may bow our heart in grief today will bow the heart in joyful worship tomorrow.

Later when news came that Jacob was ill, Joseph took his two sons with him to see his beloved father. Perhaps he wanted his sons to bear the impression of the final prophetic words of the dying saint.

Jacob first recalled to Joseph the goodness and mercy of Almighty God who had appeared to him and blessed him at Bethel. To assure the future relation of Joseph's posterity to Israel's heritage, Jacob adopted Joseph's two sons as his own. Joseph's heart was gladdened when Jacob told him that his two boys, Manasseh and Ephraim, were to be counted among the children of Israel and have a portion in the land of promise. By adopting the two grandsons, Jacob raised them to the level of his own sons. Joseph was blessed thereby as the progenitor of two of the future tribes of Israel.

His eyes dim with age, Jacob saw his two grandsons, Manasseh and Ephraim, standing nearby, but was unable to recognize them. Joseph identified the boys when Jacob questioned their identity. In response to Jacob's request Joseph brought the boys near that Jacob might bless them. Thinking of his past sorrow and present joy, Jacob exclaimed, "I had not thought to see thy face: and, lo, God hath shewed me also thy seed" (Genesis 48:11).

Bowing with respect and love to his father, Joseph led his sons closer to their grandfather. He placed the eldest next to his father's right hand that Manasseh might receive the firstborn's blessing. But Jacob crossed his arms and laid his right hand on Ephraim's head.

Jacob began his blessing with a threefold reference to God as the covenant-God, Shepherd, and Angel-Redeemer (Genesis 48:15,16).

God, before whom my fathers Abraham and Isaac did walk, the God which fed me all my life long unto this day, The Angel which redeemed me from all evil, bless the lads.

Notice the difference between this retrospect given by Jacob of his life and the earlier one given to Pharaoh that described his years as unpleasant. Jacob no longer cherished any hard thoughts about the past. His memory was filled with only the gentleness and goodness of God who had led him through his pilgrim journey.

Joseph was displeased when his father laid his right hand on Ephraim's head. He grasped his father's hand and attempted to correct the switch. Jacob's blessing, however, was given under the direction of the Spirit of God. Though nature's eyes were dim, faith's vision was sharp. Jacob refused Joseph's correction and said, "I know it, my son, I know it: he also shall become a people, and he also shall be great: but truly his younger brother shall be greater than he, and his seed shall become a multitude of nations" (Genesis 48:19).

Later Ephraim did become a much greater people than Manasseh. Ephraim occupied a position of prestige and significance from the beginning. The census lists of Numbers 1:33 and 26:37 indicate that Ephraim's descendants became a great tribe. After the Judges Ephraim became, next to Judah, the most powerful tribe in Israel.

In both his request to be buried in Canaan and his blessing upon the sons of Joseph, Jacob expressed his faith in God's Word. On his dying bed Jacob still held fast to the promises of God concerning the possession of Canaan. He said to Joseph, "Behold, I die: but God shall be with you, and bring you again unto the land of your fathers" (Genesis 48:21).

The believer is aware that his present

earthly dwelling place is only temporal. He is assured of an eternal home where he will dwell with his Lord forever. We must concern ourselves with the things that are not seen and are eternal more than with transient things of earth. We follow neither idiot hopes nor idiot fears as we obey Paul's admonition: "Therefore, my beloved brethren, be steadfast, unmoveable, always abounding in the work of the Lord, forasmuch as ye know that your labour is not in vain in the Lord" (I Corinthians 15:58).

Finding his end very near, Jacob summoned all his twelve sons to his death bed: "Gather yourselves together, and hear, ye sons of Jacob; and hearken unto Israel your father" (Genesis 49:2). In his farewell address Jacob spoke as a prophet under divine inspiration and gave significant and determinative predictions. Three features that characterize Jacob's statements are the unity of the family of Israel, the sins of individuals, and the glorious hope of the future.

Jacob spoke of each son, one by one, and described his character and prophesied what would happen to his tribe in the future. It is impossible to regard Jacob's prophetic pictures as exact representations of any one definite period in Israel's history. Some of the prophecies still await the return of the Messiah for their fulfillment.

Reuben, the eldest son, was not given the birthright because of his sin against his father (Genesis 35:22). The next two, Simeon and Levi, were set aside also because of their cruel and brutal revenge on a whole city for the sin of one man (Genesis 34:25).

A special promise was given to Judah, Jacob's fourth son. Joseph had received the twofold territorial portion, a key privilege of the birthright. But the other privileges of the birthright were solemnly transferred to Judah.

Jacob's prophecy magnified Judah in four aspects as the foremost tribe of Israel, the powerful and victorious lion-tribe, the Messianic channel, and the tribe lavishly endowed with blessings of nature. Judah's land would be abundantly blessed. He would be the chief of the tribes—"the lion"—and would grasp in his hand the scepter of a mastering warrior, king, and judge. His tribe was to be the royal tribe, the tribe of David, and ultimately the channel of the Messiah. The whole description is full of Messianic allusions.

With this announcement to Judah a new phase of Messianic prophecy was reached. The Messiah, first prophesied of the seed of Eve, then of a new nation under Abraham, is now designated to be of the tribe of Judah.

The grand prediction to Judah constitutes one of the earliest of Messianic promises: "The sceptre shall not depart from Judah, nor a lawgiver from between his feet, until Shiloh come; and to him shall the gathering of the people be" (Genesis 49:10).

"Shiloh" traditionally has been interpreted as a personal title of the Messiah that means something like "the establisher of peace." The rabbis of antiquity, though not agreeing with each other as to the meaning of the root of Shiloh, were almost unanimous in applying the term as a personal designation of the Messiah. This interpretation views Judah as reigning until the Messiah sprang out of Judah and reigned as sovereign Lord. Alfred Edersheim is one of many Christian Bible scholars who view the term as a personal title of the Messiah:

> *We state it as our deliberate conviction, that the term Shiloh can only refer to a personal designation of the Messiah, whatever the derivative meaning of the word may be.* [1]

After giving to each of the older sons a blessing appropriate to him, Jacob turned to Joseph and Benjamin. In tender tones of affection he gave Joseph the highest praise of all the sons. He gave generous recognition of Joseph's appointment by God to be a savior to Israel. As a "fruitful bough" Joseph's two tribes would enjoy extraordinary increase (cf. Deuteronomy 33:17, Joshua 17:17). The patriarch described Joseph as steadfast and triumphant over all opposition, so that he became the sustainer of Israel, "distinguished among his brothers" (Genesis 49:22-26).

Jacob's last words to his sons were charge that they bury him in the field of Machpelah in Canaan where also were buried Abraham, Sarah, Isaac, Rebekah, and Leah. Thus he declared to all his family that he would die in the same faith as Abraham. Then he peacefully drew his last breath. Jacob was gone but his spiritual legacy remained with his sons.

At Jacob's death Joseph "fell upon his father's face, and wept upon him, and kissed him" (Genesis 50:1). He mourned tenderly for the father who had mourned for him when he was taken from Canaan. Joseph called on his servants, the Egyptian physicians, to embalm his father's body to preserve it from dissolution for the long journey to Hebron.

After a public mourning of seventy days Joseph obtained Pharaoh's permission to fulfill his promise to bury his father in Canaan. In a grand funeral procession on a journey of 300 miles Joseph and his brothers were accompanied by the officers of Pharaoh's household, their own households, and all the chief men of Egypt. On the banks of the Jordan they stopped and made a sorrowful lamentation, and mourned seven days for Joseph's father (Genesis 50:10). When the people of the land saw the strangers mourning as they did, they concluded that some grievous calamity had befallen the Egyptians, and they gave the place a name that meant *the meadow, or mourning, of Egypt*.

Grief is not necessarily an indication of unbelief and hopelessness. That one sorrows in the loss of a loved one is only natural. One would experience sorrow even if the loved one were still living but leaving for a far journey, not to return for a long time. Sorrow is a natural human experience. We read of our Lord Himself at the tomb of His friend Lazarus, the shortest verse in the English Bible, "Jesus wept" (John 11:35). But on the same day that He shared the sadness of the mourning sisters, our Lord proved Himself to be "the resurrection and the life" (John 11:25) by raising Lazarus from the dead.

In steadfast hope the children of God await the resurrection. At death the soul of the believer goes to be with Christ. At the resurrection the soul is reunited with the body that is raised to glorification. Bereavement is mixed with hope in the Christian's experience. As Paul declares, we "sorrow not, even as others which have no hope. For if we believe that Jesus died and rose again, even so them also which sleep in Jesus will God bring with him" (I Thessalonians 4:13,14).

Carrying Jacob's body to Hebron was an act of faith in the future fulfillment of God's promises to Israel. Each step of the 300 mile journey was for Jacob's sons a declaration, "I believe." Their mourning was tempered with hope.

Their father was gone, and eleven brothers remained at the mercy of their brother Joseph. Immediately after they returned to Egypt, the older brothers were seized with the fear that Joseph would turn upon them and seek full revenge of their crime of selling him into slavery. Their bitter memory reigned in their hearts and poisoned their peace. They still feared that Joseph might retaliate against them after their father's death. In grief and repentance they fell down before Joseph to beg him for forgiveness. They appealed to him for mercy on the basis of the wishes of their deceased father.

Joseph was grieved that his brothers still thought him capable of taking revenge on them. He wept because it was heartbreaking to realize that his brothers had not believed him. He had matured in the area of human relationships to the extent that he would return only good for evil. Nowhere is Joseph's true character more clearly seen than in his generous treatment of his unworthy brothers. Joseph assured them that he was not their judge, and he gave them the strongest expressions of his forgiveness.

Sometimes we act toward God the way Joseph's brothers acted toward him. We fail to take Him at His Word concerning His forgiveness of our sins. He forgives completely and forever. We don't have to do anything to obtain His favor. He takes us just as we are and turns no one away.

Again Joseph lovingly reminded his brothers that God had guided in all that had happened and assured them of his continued love and provision for them. He made a classic statement that sets human circumstances in their place under the control of the sovereign purpose of God: "But as for you, ye thought evil against me, but God meant it unto good..." (Genesis 50:20). Joseph grasped the sovereignty of God over all human circumstances and refused to seek retaliation.

Joseph lived long enough to see his great-grandchildren. His age at death, 110 years, was the ideal life-span spoken of in Egyptian writings, and to the Egyptians was significant of divine blessings upon Joseph. "Life is judged not by duration," someone has said, "but by donation." Joseph was blessed with both.

Genesis reveals the following chronology of Joseph's life. He was Rachel's firstborn (30:22-24). Rachel died at Benjamin's birth (35:17,18). Joseph was age seventeen when he was sold by his brothers (37:2) and age thirty when he entered the service of Pharaoh (41:46). He revealed his identity to his brothers when he was thirty-nine, two years after the famine began. Shortly thereafter Jacob came to Egypt at age 130 (47:9), and lived there till his death at age 147 (47:28). Joseph was fifty-six years old when his father died. Joseph died at age 110 (50:26). Following his first seventeen years at home he experienced thirteen years of humiliation and then eighty years of exaltation.

Joseph's last request was the crowning expression of his faith. He repeated the promises God had made to Abraham, Isaac, and Jacob and gave the strongest proof of his faith. By his statement he disowned Egypt and chose the lot of Israel. In a noble act of faith he declared his confidence in God's fulfillment of His promise to take the people of Israel to the land of promise, and procured from his brothers an oath to bury him in Canaan: "God will surely visit you, and ye shall carry up my bones from hence" (Genesis 50:25). Hebrews 11:22 affirms this act of faith: "By faith Joseph, when he died, made mention of the departing of the children of Israel; and gave commandment concerning his bones."

The Genesis story ends with the statement regarding Joseph's temporary interment in Egypt: "So Joseph died, being an hundred and ten years old: and they embalmed him, and he was put in a coffin in Egypt" (Genesis 50:26). The narrative leaves the reader with the expectation of something more, a hope that is fulfilled in the great story of the Exodus. Genesis begins with the perfect creation of God and ends with "a coffin in Egypt." Sin wrought havoc in the world, but God set into motion a plan whereby He would redeem man, and this plan involved Israel as the channel of the Messiah.

The dates of chronologers for the duration of Israel's stay in Egypt vary greatly. Assuming the time of 400 years in Genesis 15:13 is general and the time of 430 years in Exodus 12:40 is specific in noting the time from Jacob's entry into Egypt till the Exodus, I believe the duration of Israel's stay in Egypt was 430 years.

About 360 years after Joseph's death, therefore, Israel made her exodus from Egypt and took Joseph's bones with her (Exodus 13:19). Israel carried Joseph's coffin for a thousand miles as she wandered for forty years in the wilderness between Egypt and Canaan. The mummy case in the camp of Israel was a constant reminder that God's controlling hand was working out His divine will in all Israel's struggles. As Joseph's life pointed to his Lord, his unburied body also preached and prophesied.

Some two million people were in the procession (600,000 men plus women and children, Exodus 12:37). During the time of the procession a whole generation died and was replaced by a new generation.

Even after crossing the Jordan River, Israel had to conquer and divide the land before Joseph's body could be buried. Twenty years after Israel entered the Promised Land Joseph's body was laid in its final resting place (Joshua 24:32).

Joseph should be in the *Guinness Book of World Records*! His funeral lasted the longest time and involved the largest procession of any in history. Imagine! His funeral lasted 420 years, included a 360-year temporary interment followed by a sixty-year burial march that involved two million people, outlasted an entire generation that gave way to another, followed a route of more than 1000 miles, and miraculously passed through two bodies of water on dry ground. That has to be a record! What does it all mean? It was a memorial demonstration of Joseph's faith.

In a church in Sydney, Australia, a tablet erected to the memory of a departed servant of the Lord Jesus grandly describes his life:

> *Life's work well done.*
> *Life's race well run.*
> *Life's crown well won.*

Such an epitaph could have been placed on the tomb of Joseph. Someone has said that "few people live until they die." Joseph was one who did. He experienced the blessings of God's will in his life right up to the end, and in his dying breath he uttered a final testimony of faith.

[1] Alfred Edersheim, *The Bible History—Old Testament* (Grand Rapids: William B. Eerdmans Publishing Company, 1962), Vol. 1, p. 182.